William Clark Trow

University of Michigan

Teacher
and Technology

New Designs for Learning

[

New York

APPLETON-CENTURY-CROFTS
Division of Meredith Publishing Company

FOREWORD

THE SEARCH FOR NEW LEARNING RESOURCES proceeds with increased vigor and speed. The success of improving production in business, industry, agriculture, and medicine through applications of technology, stirs the hopes of teachers, school administrators, and citizens generally that similar improvements can take place in teaching and learning.

Much educational writing is currently devoted to the advocacy or criticism of what are referred to as the new instructional media. Experimentation with and random try-out of television, teaching machines, language laboratories, and other recent developments are consuming many man-hours and much invested capital. Such efforts rarely give any indication of the relative place of each, and of the older media, in the total instructional program. Nor do they suggest the desirable procedural changes, many of which have long been needed, that are likely to result from the new mechanical and electronic innovations.

It is fortunate that a distinguished scholar in the field of educational psychology has studied these problems in the perspective of his broad and thorough knowledge of learning and teaching. William Clark Trow is professor of education and of psychology at The University of Michigan, where he is currently a member of an education committee on educational technology and of the advisory committee of the English Language Institute. In addition to his textbooks and numerous articles in the field he is a past chairman of the Division of Educational Psychology in the American Psychological Association, and past chairman of the Board of Editors of the *Journal of Educational Psychology*. He served as Director of the Army Area and Language Program of Civil Affairs Officers on the Michigan campus, and was a member of the first American Education Mission to Japan. He has taught at such widely separated points as California and Saudi Arabia. His understanding of the totality of the school program and his perceptive judgments make his analysis both timely and of special significance to all who are concerned with automation in education today and in viewing future possibilities.

I welcome this authoritative treatment by Professor Trow at a time when we need to utilize technology in every way possible that will improve learning and teaching, and when we need equally to avoid half-way measures that may not contribute to the goal of excellence.

S. M. Brownell
Superintendent of Public Schools
Detroit, Michigan

PREFACE

EDUCATIONAL TELEVISION AND TEACHING MACHINES, with the backing of commercial interests and foundation grants, have aroused a renewed interest in educational reform. The increasing school population, rising costs, and pressures of new knowledge on the already overloaded curriculum have contributed a feeling of urgency. Change is in the air. Already, new forms of school architecture, new curriculums, and new methods are being tried out at all levels from kindergarten to graduate school, and in all parts of the country and abroad. The innovations, often referred to as automation, or as technology in education, are greeted with enthusiasm by some and with apathy and even hostility by others.

In this period of impending change, there is a danger that the uninformed public will base their opinions on hearsay evidence. Otherwise intelligent people have made such public pronouncements as the following: "Television can entertain but it can't teach," "No machine will teach my child," and "Nothing can take the place of a gifted teacher."

The future historian is quite likely to discover that the educational changes beginning with the second half of the twentieth century were twofold: the rapid increase of technology in educational practice, and the concurrent re-examination and modification of the total educational program. Already the instruction provided by television and teaching machines is being subjected to more intensive scrutiny than much of the instruction it is designed to replace. The time is now ripe to examine the old as well as the new procedures, to be prepared to throw off some of the shackles which have bound the schools to the past, to introduce new and better ways, and become informed and competent guides to future progress.

It is not my purpose here to provide a how-to-do-it kit for installing television and teaching machines in a school system. These details are available from other sources, some of which are identified in footnotes and listed in the Bibliography. Instead, it is to consider the relation between the means available for instruction and their effectiveness in the different kinds of learning experiences that are provided.

A school may have decided to try some of the new media. In looking through the literature, if one finds a book or article on teaching machines, for example, there is usually no internal evidence that the author or editor has ever heard of television, and vice versa. And neither one professes any knowledge of language laboratories, team teaching, or flexibility in classroom size. This is no criticism of the books and articles, but it does suggest some of the difficulties educators face in their efforts to profit from the new media.

There are, of course, a few exceptions—particularly the writings of James D. Finn, J. Lloyd Trump, and some others—but these are somewhat disturbing in their bold prophecies and lack of explanations. My purpose in this volume is to consider the need for and possibilities of grouping the various media into a common-sense pattern of instruction which is workable and which will do a better educational job than could otherwise be done.

Following the introductory chapter, Chapter 2 reviews some of the many things we know about learning, and Chapter 3, the technology we already have. Both are presented in such a way as to suggest better ways to provide the kind of environmental control we call *teaching*. Chapter 4 is a continuation of Chapter 3: it deals with environmental control, but introduces the two chief technological innovations, television and teaching machines. Then in Chapter 5, possible implications are considered on the basis of the systems approach that is part of the new technology. In Chapter 6, I have attempted to draw a realistic picture of the way things might look in operation.

My purpose, therefore, is first to view instructional media, both new and old, in the light of their historical development. The new technology will thus be seen to be a natural outgrowth of the old and familiar in the direction of better teaching and learning. But new concepts will be required and new demands will be made on educators at all levels before it will make the contribution it can make, not to American schools alone, but to the enlightenment of mankind.

W.C.T.

CONTENTS

1

The Educational
Enterprise

EDUCATION THE WORLD OVER is a stupendous enterprise and one that is continuing to grow. In the United States alone, according to figures recently released by the Office of Education, enrollment in the public schools in 1950 was 25 million while in 1960 it was 36 million, with an expected 50 million by 1970. They were operated (1959–60) at a total cost of $15.6 billion, an increase of $2 billion in two years. During the same two years the instructional staff increased approximately 10 per cent, to nearly a million and a half persons.

These last are the people who operate the schools and who, directly and indirectly, will determine in large measure what each of the millions of children and young people will be required to do in school, and what means will be employed for their education. Great numbers of them are deeply concerned, dedicated people bringing their knowledge, skill, and creative powers to bear on the educational problems which confront them, laboring with a devotion that is often beyond the call of duty. But all are human and subject to human

1

frailties, and some are handicapped by insufficient knowledge and skill and by attitudes and prejudices derived from limited background and experience. Moreover, they are subjected to pressures of special interests, and they are habituated to procedures which have continued long after their usefulness has ended and obsolescence has set in.

THE NEW MEDIA

In such an enormously complex enterprise, it is to be expected that innovations would come slowly. But changes have been made. Population increases have had their effect, as have new psychological and educational theories. And more recently, the rapid developments in human knowledge, particularly in the sciences, have thrown added burdens on the school curriculum, as have the tumultuous political events occurring day-by-day as new nations are assuming the responsibilities of self-government. There is much more to learn than ever before, especially since modern communication and transportation have brought the knowledge of these events to our doorstep. And now new technological changes are actually forcing their way into our school buildings and threatening to upset the procedures which have been long hallowed by custom.

Technology—Revolution or Evolution?

Are educational television and teaching machines, to say nothing of language laboratories, team teaching, different sized classrooms, going to produce marked changes in education, or are they merely passing fads? Will they disrupt, depersonalize, and overstandardize education, or will they serve to improve it? Will electronics and automation banish teachers from the schools to become victims of technological unemployment?

Those who are concerned about such questions as these, and who view with alarm the signs of technological change in education, are likely to think of *technology* as synonymous with *machinery*. They fear that the human personal relationships, such as they are, will be lost in schools which substitute machines for teachers. The word *technology* does not refer necessarily to machines, as many seem to think, but to any practical art using scientific knowledge. Etymologically the word derives from the Greek *technikos*, from *technē*, an art. The Latin form is *texere*, to weave or construct, from which we have such words as *text*, *textile*, and *architect*. The basic concept is thus a pattern or construct of interrelated parts. True this is what a machine is, in part, but so is a school system. And what educators are concerned with is the study of school systems and of the modifications that can be made in them to attain the desired educational objectives.

Educational changes have been made in the past, and it is certain that they will continue to be made in the future. But their results will be less a revolution, as some have predicted, than an acceleration in the tempo of evolution, probably somewhat similar to what took place during the first quarter of the present century. Those were the days when psychology began to develop tests and to perform experiments in learning and transfer which destroyed the earlier complacency about formal discipline, and when it contributed psychoanalytic, behavioristic, and Gestalt concepts to education. Philosophy emphasized learning by doing and the whole child. Problem and project methods in part superseded the Herbartian five formal steps, and the junior high school found new ways of dealing with an earlier population explosion in the schools. They were great days. Since then, with our preoccupation with two world wars with a depression sandwiched in between, evolution has proceeded more slowly, consolidating gains and preparing to embark on new ventures.

Skeptics and Prophets

New ways have their enemies as well as their friends. Skeptics viewing the new educational technology shake their heads or make bombastic pronouncements. A very self-confident although not too well-informed assistant professor of English sounded off in this way: "But it is absurd to believe that any machine (including TV) can teach as well as an intelligent and well-trained human being who enjoys doing so . . . The net effect of the machine approach to education is to separate the student from books even more than he already is." And a state commissioner of education was reported in the press as announcing that "the alluring but misleading image of the so-called master teacher performing before the camera" results in "impersonalized, dehumanized teaching and an increase in distance between pupil and teacher."

It will be possible to evaluate such statements as these better after we have explored the situation. Suffice it to say at this point, first, that in spite of the enthusiastic prophecies about the future of automation there is here no intention of banishing teaching personnel from the schools; and second, that it may be desirable, at times, to maintain some distance between teachers and pupils as is now done when the latter read in the library or do their homework. The importance of the "living teacher" is not questioned, but only his competence in the various roles he is expected to play.

For the moment a report from a living and presumably personalized and humanized mathematics teacher is not without pertinence: "I explained a point very carefully," he said, "but the class didn't get it so I went over it a second time, and still they didn't understand it. Then when I explained it the third time, I understood it." This teacher was more frank than some. Pupils should be spared such incompetence. People generally do not know what goes on in most classrooms, but television and teaching machine programs are carefully prepared and are public. What they are teaching is known and it can at least be assumed that the kinescopes, video tapes, and programmed materials are made by people who know what they are talking about.

Some shudder at the thought of the school as an automated track like an assembly line in which the elements of learning are, so to speak, sprayed or bolted on to the pupils as they move slowly toward graduation. As a matter of fact, this is a better description of the present system of instruction than anything contemplated by the new technology. All, or nearly all students now move forward at the same speed a grade at a time. But there is a difference: in the assembly line each unit receives what is needful when it is needed. Units are not grouped together in various stages of completion with all of them receiving the same treatment whether they are ready for it or not. Actually, many current innovations are aimed directly at the problem of individualizing instruction much more than is now possible in the familiar one-teacher-to-one-room system in which the children in each grade proceed like ships in a convoy, the fastest and the slowest all compelled to move ahead at the same speed.

Some have pointed to education as the last of the great human enterprises to be influenced by technology. Certainly agriculture, mining, manufacturing, and the military have been relatively quick to take advantage of new discoveries and inventions and new techniques. Already business and industrial organizations are using the new media in training their employees, particularly for assembly and sales work. The federal government is the largest customer, and the armed forces have devised and purchased many kinds of expensive equipment to aid in training recruits and others in new skills. It has been urged that the new media are well adapted to training in vocational and other skills, but that they are inadequate in the face of the wider goals of education. The answer is simple. If they are not effective in meeting educational objectives they should not be used for that purpose. But many skills need to be acquired in the process of becoming educated, not only sensorimotor skills but also mathematical and language skills and others. That medium should be selected, whether "new" or "old," that most adequately meets the educational objectives of any part of any school subject.

Outside of the public schools nearly 60 million adults are even now engaged in some form of educational activity. Instruction is going on not only in regular university courses but also by extension and correspondence. Many agencies besides industry and the armed forces are participating—labor unions, libraries and museums, clubs, parent associations, religious organizations, and others. The world population, now nearly 3 billion, is expected to double by the year 2000. Whether it does or not, the new technology offers exciting possibilities for providing more and better education for the vast audience of adults as well as for the children and youth.

But no *revolution* is expected, except as the word is used as a figure of speech, a hyperbole, to refer to possible new adjustments, a kind of temporary speeding up of the evolutionary process. Audio-visual materials, including television, are in reality but an extension of the picturebook of Comenius; the programmed teaching machines, of the workbook and the teacher's oral explanation; the language laboratories, of the native speaker; and team teaching, of departmentalized instruction. Projected changes in school architecture accord, as they should, with the well-established dictum, form follows function.

But to say that the new technology is but an extension of the old is only in part true. It is like saying that the automobile and the airplane are but extensions of the horse. Both are more efficient means of transportation for most purposes; however, over the years they have wrought enormous changes not only in transportation but in many other aspects of the culture. These changes may constitute a revolution, but rapid as they appear in historical perspective, to those who have lived through the period they have seemed quite gradual—and satisfying—instead of being upsetting.

Perhaps the greatest advantage accruing from the advance of technology into the realm of education is the occasion it provides for a careful scrutiny of educational objectives and techniques. Just what is education trying to do? And what are the best ways of doing it?

EDUCATIONAL OBJECTIVES

The objectives of education have been stated in many ways, each carrying important implications for curriculum and method. To many they seem obvious enough: to teach the standard school subjects—reading, arithmetic, French, physics, and so on. But if the further question is asked, Why teach these subjects? the answers begin to vary: to transmit the cultural heritage, to impart knowledge, to train the mind, to enable people to satisfy their needs, to serve the state. In any case, the objective seems to be to help children (and adults) to learn, even though there are differences of opinion as to what they should learn and how they should be taught.

Means and Ends

It is of first importance that the means should not determine the ends. We should certainly not base our curriculum on what can be taught by television or teaching machines, or for that matter, by books or projects. This would be a prime example of getting the cart before the horse. Both old and new methods must be scrutinized to discover the best ways to attain the objectives sought. Similarly the curriculum itself needs continuing evaluation. Is there a proper balance between the emphasis on subject matter and on emotional and social adjustment, between academic and vocational subjects, between the traditional disciplines and the complex controversial issues of the contemporary world?

It is, of course, futile to prescribe the same treatment for everybody, but it is possible to hold to the ideal that each child shall have the opportunity to attain his potential level of development. On the academic side, there can well be a common effort in matters of communication, and in an understanding of numerical and spatial relationships. In other areas, individual interests, aptitudes, and needs must be the determining factors. For those who know anything about the differences in the intellectual abilities of children, to say nothing of the processes of learning and forgetting, the familiar attempts to prescribe the number of years that should be devoted by all to any one subject is little short of ridiculous.

The Human Imperatives

There are certain necessary ultimate objectives, however, which are common to mankind. Human society, through its various agencies and organizations, has not been overly successful in teaching itself how to attain these objectives. If, as someone has said, the trouble with the younger generation is the older generation, the reason is that neither by instruction, precept, nor example have the elders been able to train the young to accommodate themselves rationally to the three human imperatives within the framework of which all find themselves encaged: man must live; man must live with others; and man must live with himself.[1]

Man must live. If he does not remain alive, all else is of no avail. Educationally this imperative demands a program of health, physical education, and recreation. It implies safety education—in school, on the playground, in the shop, in the street, and on the highways. But since man must eat to live,

[1] Harold P. Marley, "When Humanism Becomes a Religion," *The Humanist,* IV (Spring, 1944), 24–26.

and to eat he must earn, provision for vocational training and assistance in vocational adjustment are responsibilities shared by the schools with other institutions and with industry. Whatever the arrangements, instruction is needed, and that instruction can probably be made more effective than it is at present. It includes not only shop experience but also technical training and engineering and the steps in preparation for the professions, whether in science and mathematics, the arts and humanities, in law or medicine, or any other. The health and vocation objectives cannot be disregarded if man is to live.

Man must live with others. A recent editorial in a magazine of wide circulation described the contribution of two or three of the world's geniuses, and then for a punch line, asked how these men would have profited from courses in adjustment to the group. True, many acquire the attitudes and skills needed for satisfactory interpersonal relationships and the enjoyment of group living as a consequence of their home experiences and others which reinforce desirable behavior, but many do not. As a consequence, there are those who find satisfaction in murder and violence and in minor forms of antisocial conduct, in stealing and cheating and in racial prejudice and discrimination. Many have not learned to communicate in ways that result in mutual understanding. One occasionally hears of adults who do not speak to each other, sometimes members of the same family. Some have not learned to cooperate with others in the countless formal and informal ways that are necessary in any society, or they fail to receive appointments and promotions they seek because they simply cannot get along with other people.

Whether in separate courses, or by new educational methods and activities, or through its psychological services, the school has ways of helping pupils to live with others. Not only in the conquest of crime and in the "waging of peace" among nations, but in more common ways, people need to learn better ways of getting along together. In a democracy, the citizen participates in many activities outside the field of his vocational or professional specialization. Clubs, committees, commissions, conferences, boards, and councils abound, as well as assemblies and legislatures, and in them much of the world's work is done, and decisions great and small are made which affect not only the participants, but many others as well. Leadership qualities are widely sought. The participation and citizenship objective cannot be disregarded, for man must live with others.

Man must live with himself. This is perhaps the most difficult of all. The pursuit of happiness is conjoined with life and liberty in the American constitution as one of the rights to which man is entitled, and in the attainment of which government is expected to assist. The schools as an agency of government have a peculiar responsibility in this respect. Just as the more extreme failures among those who cannot live with others are to be found in the police courts, the jails, prisons, and penitentiaries, so the failures of those who have not learned to live with themselves are to be found in the numerous mental institutions, on the couches of psychiatrists and psychoanalysts, in the offices of the clinical psychologists and social agencies, in the consulting rooms of the clergy, and even among the philosophically inclined who are in search of "the meaning of life." Many have adopted adjustment mechanisms that are irrational and self-defeating. They are at war with themselves.

We do not expect the school to change all this, say, with a little course on "How to live with yourself." But the school program can be aimed to develop wholesome personalities rather than their opposite. Its tasks can be so adapted to the learners that they arouse interest, hope, even enthusiasm, instead of aggression, anxiety, or despair. To this end school psychologists, counsellors, and visiting teachers can help in the adaptation of the curriculum to the individual needs and abilities of pupils and help them with their personal problems. But all the professional personnel are in one way or another responsible for contributing to the objective of satisfaction and happiness, for man must be able to live with himself.

Objectives and Values

This statement of educational objectives is at a high level of generality, as philosophical statements of human values are likely to be. Perhaps one of the most useful list of values was developed by Eduard Spranger:

Cognitive—knowing, thinking
Aesthetic—feeling, artistic appreciation and enjoyment
Political—recognition, power
Religious—immanent and transcendental mysticism
Economic—seeking the products of labor, vocation
Social—serving others, altruism

While religious values are the concern of other social institutions, health values are in part the concern of the schools. With these changes, if a proper balance is maintained among the values so that no one is carried to such an excess that it destroys any of the others, the list provides interesting and useful guidelines for the efforts not only of individuals but also of institutions.

A somewhat different list of objectives was early suggested by Herbert Spencer,[2] who recommended that the then common emphases on educational goals be turned upside down:

Accomplishments, the fine arts, *belle-lettres,* and all those things which, as we say, constitute the efflorescence of civilization, should be wholly subordinate to that [scientific] knowledge and discipline in which civilization rests. *As they occupy the leisure part of life, so should they occupy the leisure part of education. . . .* What knowledge is of most worth? Science

[2] Herbert Spencer, *Education: Intellectual, Moral, Physical,* Ch. I, "What Knowledge Is of Most Worth?" (New York, D. Appleton and Company, 1861), pp. 93–94.

For direct self-preservation, or the maintenance of life and health . . .

For that indirect self-preservation which we call gaining a livelihood . . .

For the due discharge of parental functions . . .

For that interpretation of national life, past and present, without which the citizen cannot rightly regulate his conduct . . .

For the most perfect production and highest enjoyment of art in all its forms . . .

For purposes of discipline—intellectual, moral and religious

Another famous list [3] which has influenced many subsequent compilations is the "cardinal objectives" of education: health, command of fundamental processes, worthy home membership, vocation, civic education, worthy use of leisure, and ethical character. Many other lists have been presented more recently, among them that of Launor F. Carter: [4] imparting subject matter, training in thinking and creativity, developing skills and techniques, developing attitudes, socializing, physical development, and child care.

In these lists, a transition from educational content to mental and behavioral processes will be noted. But such general statements of objectives leave the specific goals, the more immediate objectives to be worked out. For example, what geographical, historical, or scientific facts should be included in the curriculum? And at what age or grade levels, if it is the expectation of the schools that they transmit knowledge (or the cultural heritage)? Other immediate goals raise the question, What emphasis will be placed on various cognitive experiences (for example, memorizing, judging, and reasoning) to satisfy the common demand that the schools

[3] Commission on the Reorganization of Secondary Education, *Cardinal Principles of Secondary Education,* U.S. Office of Education, Bull. 35, 1918.

[4] Launor F. Carter, "The Challenge of Automation in Education," in John E. Coulson, ed., *Programmed Learning and Computer-Based Instruction* (New York, John Wiley & Sons, Inc., 1962), pp. 3–12.

train young people to think? And how will attitudes, social behavior, and responsibility be emphasized so that the schools may contribute to individual and social adjustment, and to the ideal of good citizenship? A well-developed technology can presumably make improvements all along the line. But evaluations must be made not only by comparing the new with the old, but also by comparing both with the ideal of what might be.

Specific Objectives

In programmed instruction, specific objectives must be identified and made explicit; indeed such specificity is desirable in any kind of instruction. The programmer must be able to answer the question, What must the learner be able to do in order to demonstrate that he has learned what he is expected to learn?

Some time ago a professor of history went to the office of a measurement specialist to seek his assistance in composing an objective-type examination for his history course. The specialist asked him, "What are your course objectives?" The historian replied with some asperity, "Why, to give the students a knowledge of history, of course!" He went on to say that if the specialist had to ask a question like that, it was clear that he was not competent to give advice in such matters, and he left the office in disgust.

Programming has turned a spotlight on the guessing game students have long been forced to play, a game in which as one student reported of one of his teachers, "The book is about one thing, the lectures are about another, and the examination is on something else again!" The students have one cue if they can find out whether the examination is "objective or essay type," and another if there are two or more examinations, so they can come to know the kind of questions the instructor asks.

But programming is instruction, not testing, and it is assumed, other things being equal, that students will learn what they are taught. It follows then that they should be taught what they are expected to learn. They and the teacher should know beforehand what kind of evidence will be used to determine whether or not they have learned what they are expected to have learned. With a performance objective, the criteria can be stated simply, for example, to type so many words a minute, to construct a working model, or to run a mile in so many minutes. Performances like these are observable and measurable. But to know the facts of history, to understand how a radio works, or to appreciate good literature, while all commendable as objectives, are lacking in specificity. It is possible to state objectives in such a way that there will be agreement as to whether or not they have been attained. There can be such agreement when the objectives are stated in terms of observable behavior—what the student is expected to be able to *do, say,* or *write,* that is, his terminal behavior.

When introducing statements of objectives, such words as *to know, to understand, to appreciate, to grasp the significance of,* and *to enjoy* are open to many interpretations.[5] *To write, to recite, to construct, to list, to compare,* and *to contrast* can be interpreted less freely, and the words following these would refer to limited units of instruction—the behavior the learners would be expected to exhibit as evidence of achievement when they have completed the program.

Two further conditions are important. One is to state the means the student will have at his disposal, for example, a slide rule, a dictionary, a list from which to choose correct items, printed or spoken stimuli (i.e., translation or conversation in a foreign language), and so on. The other condition is the indication of minimum expectations—a time or distance

[5] For a partially programmed elucidation, see Robert F. Mager, *Preparing Objectives for Programmed Instruction* (San Francisco, Fearon Publishers, Inc., 1961).

limit, for example, or number or percent of items that must be recalled. The criterion may have to be arbitrarily defined, as when the objective involves a qualitative judgment of originality, a critical attitude, leadership ability, or excellence of performance in art and music. Sometimes ranked samples of performance in such areas can be constructed and the expected level identified. In any case a conscientious effort to identify the criteria expected at different stages of instruction has the advantage of improving instruction and adapting it to the varying abilities of different learners.

Between the broad, generalized objectives referring to life values and the narrow, specific objectives in teaching a particular unit of subject matter lies a wide area of uncertainty. Three questions reveal the nature of the problems in this area: What subjects shall be taught? What parts of each subject shall be emphasized? and What parts shall be taught at different age and grade levels?

Sometimes one hears it said that for the answers to such questions one must go to philosophy because science can only answer the question, How?, but not the question, What? This is one of the most pernicious half truths with which mankind is afflicted. To say that science can show how to teach but not what to teach is much like saying that it can say how to eat but not what to eat. While ultimate values are certainly matters of philosophical speculation, there are nearly as many answers as there are philosophers. If it is agreed, whether or not with the help of a philosopher, that in the present culture arithmetic skills are needed, only scientific inquiry can determine what arithmetic skills should be taught, to whom, and when. This inquiry would include surveys of the uses of arithmetic, hypotheses concerning difficulty and concerning pupil growth and interest, experimental testing of these hypotheses, and modification of the procedure in the light of the results, including their effect on more generalized abilities such as concept formation and critical thinking. Judgments must be made before all the facts are in, and as new facts are discovered, modifications must be made accordingly.

All this is familiar enough and is satisfactory as far as it goes. But in the past it has resulted in egregious error because answers were often sought to the wrong question, that is, What arithmetic (or other subject) should be *taught?* Instead, the question should be, What arithmetic (or other subject) should be *learned?* The difference is often not recognized, but it is of tremendous importance.

As things now stand, texts, units, workbooks, teacher guides, and all the rest are assembled, and with careful planning, the *teacher* has covered the course by the end of the year. The pupils have been exposed to it, but everything is carefully arranged so that the majority will not learn what has been taught. They are neatly catalogued in previously prepared positions labeled *B, C, D, E,* and *F!* And to make matters worse, nobody really knows what these pupils actually know and what they don't know. How long this expensive and futile procedure will continue it is difficult to say.

If it is not necessary for students to know what they have been taught but have not learned, time and effort are being wasted in trying to teach it to them. If it is necessary knowledge and skill they lack, then means should be employed to enable them to acquire it. Fortunately the new media provide these means. The problem for the experts is to agree on what is necessary knowledge and skill. This should be less difficult, say, in mathematics and foreign languages than in science and the social studies. For the latter, as an example, it may be that out of a thousand facts about a certain country, any hundred would be sufficient at a given age level, and the choice could be left to the student. But he should not be given a *C* for not knowing five hundred facts. He can learn more later.

A Better Education Is Possible

The educational task ahead is to correct at least some of the errors of the past and not try to build on them. We can no longer be content with the easy, half-way measures that have long been taken for granted. Education can now approach its objectives, both near and remote, more closely than ever before because it can now adapt to the individual needs of all. Many of the deficiencies of those people from a deprived cultural background can be corrected. Variations in personality and temperament can be recognized and the curricular demands modified accordingly. Differences in ability can be measured and appropriate educational tasks prescribed.

Variations in the methods of group instruction, grading, and promotion have been tried out in the hope of improving things. Sometimes, when some modifications in method are made experimentally, no significant differences are found, say in average test scores. In such cases it is customary to conclude that no change is needed, that the situation is all right. But there is another possibility: both methods may be unsatisfactory. Hence complacency with the old is out of place as is disinterest in the new. In the early days of the automobile, owners were sometimes advised to get a horse, but this did not discourage the automobile industry. The new technology has the potentiality for improvement that does not reside in the old. But it is only a means. The effectiveness of the means depends on the skill of those who employ them. It is therefore important to consider not only the educational goals sought but also what is actually involved in learning and teaching.

2

The Learner and his Environment

WHAT DOES A PERSON DO WHEN HE LEARNS? Various learning theories, although they differ in details, have much in common. The description which follows, therefore, will briefly explore the common ground. In this exploration, those with recent psychological training will recognize much that is familiar. But the view is an extremely useful one since it provides a basis for predictions concerning the effectiveness of old and new media alike, and of the desirability of any proposed technological changes.

THE DYNAMIC ORGANISM

While it is well known that the learner is not a mere passive receptacle into which knowledge may be poured, some school instruction is carried on as if this were an adequate description of the learning process. Instead, the learner is a dynamic, self-activated organism. He not only *is,* but *does.* What does he do?

The Learner Matures

Given satisfactory nurture (food, clothing, and shelter, and an adequate social environment), the infant grows according to his inherited nature. The word *develop* is frequently used in this connection, but the meaning is often confused since it is used both intransitively (the child develops), and transitively (the school develops the child). In spite of the confusion resulting from this double usage, given an adequate environment, children do grow toward maturity following certain natural growth sequences. They must walk before they can run, as the saying goes. From studies of child growth and development it has been discovered that many of the age-old educational problems of instruction and of maintaining discipline arise not because of total or even partial depravity of the child, but because school tasks have been set for children which they are not sufficiently mature to perform. Because there is a six- or seven-year span of ability in any one grade, schools have made valiant efforts to adapt their offerings to such differences, to begin where the pupil is, to pace the instruction sequentially at the rate different pupils can travel, and to provide opportunities for them to select from their environment what they need for their development. But such efforts, understandably, have not been so successful as could be wished.

The Learner Seeks

There is some advantage in employing growth theory as briefly outlined above, for it forces the recognition that an adult-ordered curriculum may be quite unsatisfactory, that the learner, like the customer, is always right in the sense that it is his abilities, interests, and needs that largely determine what he can and will do—not the ideas of scholars or even of curriculum committees. Programming for the new media takes this principle seriously. An environment that merely provides the opportunity for a child to make the right responses, however, is not enough. Because of his immaturity he needs professional help in making the necessary discriminations—both in the aspects of the environment to which to respond, and in the responses to be made—if his needs are to be satisfied and the educational goals attained.

The Learner Perceives

Perceptions are necessarily mediated by the several senses which report conditions and changes in the internal and external world. The sensory mechanism, however, does not report all, e.g., magnetic fields and infra-red light, and it may be defective. Sensory defects should be discovered and if possible, corrected, in order to promote valid expectancies concerning an individual's competence. Greater sensory acuity apparently cannot be developed by training, but sharper perceptual discriminations can be.

When a person perceives, he identifies things and, using his memory, recurring patterns of things. Perception is a complex process. Narrowly defined it refers only to sensory experiences but it involves inner cognitive processes as well. Among these are recall, identification, recognition, discrimination, comparison and contrast, and conceptualization. Without recall one could presumably perceive structure in the external world, but with it he can recognize a sensory pattern as something he has seen or heard before. He can identify it whether or not he can give it a name. Further, he can compare or contrast it with similar experiences and thus discriminate between them and their concomitant variations. And so, often with the aid of formal instruction, he learns to build up concepts and attach names to what he perceives. However, a concept is not dependent on any present or immediately perceived situation.

The Learner Responds

(As a consequence of inner drive or of inner or outer stimulation, the learner responds.)The behavior is more complicated than we usually realize, made up as it is of external or overt components (action that can be observed by others), and of internal or covert components (neuromuscular and glandular responses), some of which can be observed introspectively as feelings, emotions, ideas, or attitudes. Even these may reveal themselves overtly in facial expression or bodily movement or eventuate in overt goal-directed behavior. The stimulating parts of the environment, using the language of those who work with electronic computers, are sometimes referred to as the "input," and the response the "output."

Thus the input [1] consists of any external stimulus events whether chance or planned that have a bearing on the performance of a task. A task is any group of activities that are performed about the same time or in close sequence and have the same work objective. Thus a task may take a few minutes or weeks, though smaller divisions are sometimes referred to as subtasks.

The response is overt. It may, however, be the outcome of considerable inner or covert activity, generally referred to as the cognitive processes. These have been analyzed in considerable detail,[2] but for convenience they can be included under four heads: knowing, understanding, generalizing, and

[1] The ensuing definitions in somewhat modified form are derived from Robert B. Miller, "Analysis and Specification of Behavior for Training," in Robert Glaser, ed., *Training Research and Education* (Pittsburgh, University of Pittsburgh Press, 1962), and from Robert M. Gagné, "Human Functions in Systems," and Robert B. Miller, "Task Description and Analysis," both in Robert M. Gagné, ed., *Psychological Principles in System Development* (New York, Holt, Rinehart and Winston, Inc., 1962).

[2] Benjamin S. Bloom, ed., *Taxonomy of Educational Objectives— The Classification of Educational Goals* (New York, Longmans, Green & Co., 1956).

problem solving. In brief, knowing is the process that has long been the chief concern of educational institutions. It can be thought of as the recall of concepts or propositions through associative connections. Facts are essential, but they are inert and worthless if they are not used either for the enjoyment they provide or for the practical services they can render. Numerous experiments have shown that knowledge of subject matter is no guarantee that it will be used in new situations. A needed fact may not be perceived as such when embedded in another pattern of things or events, the relationships of separate experiences may not be seen, and an earlier set may continue to operate when the situation changes. In short, [previous experiences cannot be expected to transfer to new situations. It is therefore necessary to teach the kind of behavior sought, whatever the medium employed.]

Understanding is a special kind of knowledge, that of the nature of relationships of various kinds between concepts— spatial, temporal, causal, etc. A person who understands knows enough about objects and events so he can predict what will happen when they are brought together in different combinations and when transferred to different contexts. Generalizing is a process of inductively including different items under the same concept categories (stimulus generalization) or of varying the responses to the same stimulus situation (response generalization).[Problem solving involves all the above processes employed in order to perform some task for which the organism has no instinctive or learned mode of response.]The process has been extensively studied in recent years under the rubric, decision making.

All these acts may be carried on internally, but they are known chiefly through the medium of language. The subject gives a verbal report. Or he may perform certain tasks that reveal the outcome of his mental activities. In either case, the process is sometimes referred to as interpreting, and is defined as identifying the meaning of inputs, that is, describing them in terms of their effects instead of their appearances, as is done in perception.

The response may therefore take one of three forms: communication, product, and performance. Communication in this connection refers to the verbal report, a code by means of which the nature of the covert response may be revealed. The product is the form taken in communicating the interpretation, that is, the outcome of thinking however communicated. Critical and creative thinking have recently been receiving considerable attention. Criticism, or evaluation, and creativity, or invention, are two important forms of interpretation. A performance is any response, but the meaning here is restricted to situations in which the emphasis is on some perceptual-motor skill whether in pressing keys on a machine, inserting a part on an assembly line, pole-vaulting, or driving an automobile. They include the bodily skills of the athletic field, the hand skills—primarily vocational and artistic—and the vocal skills of singing and speaking. All can, of course, be improved with practice and instruction. Sometimes the action is brief, like shooting at a target, sometimes it is a part skill like batting, and sometimes it is a longer continuing process like writing, playing a game, painting a picture, or playing a musical instrument.

The Learner Remembers

By means of complex neural processes previous experiences of the organism are recorded, whether or not they are consciously recalled, and so serve to influence later perceptions and responses. The memory trace may be in the form of a set or habit derived from previous responses. The child responds in ways he has been told to respond or in ways in which he has responded before, but he may be quite unaware of these influences, or they may be verbalized and be made with a clear awareness of what has previously occurred.

A number of different factors influence retention. Physiologists emphasize electrochemical action, heredity, and brain injury; association psychologists, contiguity, recency, frequency, intensity, and reinforcement; gestaltists, the pattern of relationships; and Freudians, repressions and the influence of attitudes, complexes, and cathexes. Probably all of these factors are influential, but whatever the mechanism, memory is an important variable. Educationally it is desirable that the learner remember the correct responses, and that he remember to make them when they are appropriate.

Instruction thus involves the control of the learner's environment in part by the presentation of successive stimulus situations to the learner (input) in such a way that he will respond in certain ways that are considered desirable by the instructor, the learner, or both, and that lead in the direction of certain goals or immediate objectives.

The Learner Attains

A goal may be a simple one, as when a youngster succeeds in getting food into his mouth, or an archer hits the target, or a student answers a question or solves a problem. He may fail or be only partially successful, in which case learning proceeds perhaps by further trials, or perhaps by moving toward simpler intermediate goals. When the goal is attained the unit of behavior comes to an end, to be followed by others, all of which presumably lead to the more remote objectives.

The key points in the learner's behavior that have been briefly indicated can be diagrammed for convenience as in Figure 1.

THE CONTROLLING ENVIRONMENT

Any organism is, of course, entirely dependent on its environment, which must contain the components necessary for its existence, or it will die. Even if it is merely deprived of external sensory stimulation, to the extent that this is experi-

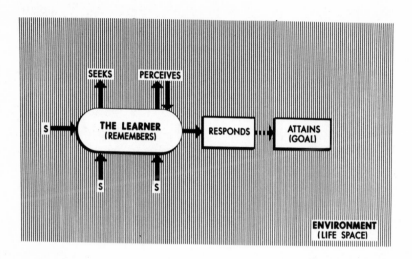

FIGURE 1. The Dynamic Organism. The learner and his activities are contained within a surrounding environment, or those parts of it which in any way bear upon him, and are referred to as his life space. Various stimuli (*S, S, S*), impinge on the organism which actively *seeks* satisfying conditions, *perceives* certain parts of the environmental situation, *remembers* previous experiences, *responds,* and as a consequence in some cases attains its goal.

mentally possible, strange psychological phenomena occur which would be likely to be followed by dementia if the experiments should be continued. The physical and social environment of a society affects its food habits, occupations, recreations, attitudes, and even its political and religious beliefs. Theoretically a complete control of the environmental life space could produce any kind of culture the controllers might desire. For various reasons, however, such complete control is not possible in the foreseeable future.[3] For the present, suf-

[3] George Orwell's *1984* (New York, Harcourt, Brace & World, Inc., 1949) and B. F. Skinner's *Walden II* (New York, The Macmillan Company, 1948) seek to forecast such a society but under different kinds of controls. See also C. R. Rogers and B. F. Skinner, "Some Issues Concerning the Control of Human Behavior—a Symposium," *Science,* 124 (November 30, 1956) 1060–1064.

ficient control is necessary to enable people of any age to learn what they need and want to learn more effectively than has been hitherto possible. After this brief examination of what the learner does, the next logical step is to inspect his contacts with the environment.

Three Worlds

For convenience the environment can be divided into three parts—the world of things, of people, and of symbols. The world of things is the objective world that is all about us, the world which natural scientists have studied with the result that accurate predictions can be made concerning it. As perceived, it is composed of objects which have been classified in various ways as animal, vegetable, and mineral and as constructs such as houses, bridges, tools, and so on. Children must learn to behave so as not to be hurt by these things, and to use them, manipulate them, or reconstruct them in new patterns.

The world of people is ourselves. The individual, the family, the peer group, the organization, the society—these have their peculiar ways that novelists, philosophers, and social scientists have observed and studied, and about which they have been somewhat less successful in making predictions. Individual likes and dislikes make it difficult to learn to live with people, and the almost indeterminate effects they have on each other are a major influence in the success or failure in any human enterprise. Those who oppose the use of teaching machines make much of the personal influences of the gifted teacher, and they are no doubt correct. But even though many teachers are not particularly gifted, interpersonal relationships are still very important.

Beginning with the earliest efforts of the child to understand the spoken word, the world of symbols, both verbal and numerical, takes over an increasing fraction of the learner's time and interest. The prolonged discussions about the curriculum suggest that this is the only world with which the schools should be concerned. While it is necessary to be able to deal with symbols and to spend a large amount of time in learning to do so, this ability should be recognized as only the means by which man can learn to live, to live with others, and live with himself in the world of things and people. He must somehow learn to think more rationally than he has yet done, to communicate more effectively, and to act more intelligently. The schools must do even a better job than they have in the past of teaching their students to look and say, to think and do.

Educational theorists have long concerned themselves with these responsibilities, and as a consequence the modern school is a far better place to learn than was its medieval prototype. Rousseau dramatized the importance of the natural environment and the inquiring mind, and Pestalozzi, of affectionate —even familial—pupil-teacher relationships and the advantage in using symbolic materials to move from the simple and concrete to the complex and abstract. Herbart designed a pattern for inductive teaching. Froebel emphasized perceptual discrimination and manipulation, child growth and development, and pupil activity. His *Kindergarten* he first called a *Kleinkinderbeschäftigungsanstalt,* a fortunate revision, but the term means a small children's activity institution. With this background, education was ready, or almost ready, for Spencer's question, "What knowledge is of most worth?" and for Dewey's accent on self-expression, participation, problem solving, and the broadening of educational values.

The task is a continuing one of arranging the environment of the dynamic organism, the growing child, in such ways that he can learn effectively to live in his three worlds of things, people, and symbols. Psychological knowledge makes it possible to break down the learning process into its more obvious parts and deal with each one separately.

Stimulus Input

Sometimes it is impossible to say just what the perceived stimulus is that produces a response. Often the principle of multiple causation must be invoked, and in such cases the organism is said merely to emit a response. It is known that merely reinforcing certain emitted responses tends to increase the probability of their repetition under similar conditions, or to produce progressively closer approximations to the desired or criterion performance.[4] It is often possible, however, to identify the stimulus or cue that sets off the response. Such cues are derived from various sources in the internal and external environment, from chance environmental conditions as well as from the feedback, the consequences of previous responses, whether or not they are given or indicated by an instructor.

With the multitude of stimuli constantly bombarding the sensorium, it is natural that there would be some kind of selective process. The process is called attention. The computer people refer to it by the picturesque term, *filtering*.

If a student is to respond correctly, he must learn to filter out the irrelevant stimuli and respond to the relevant, the appropriate pattern of things and events in the three worlds which surround him. He must learn to perceive the significant, whether it is a dot, a line, a pattern of lines, colors, sounds, etc., and he must learn to discriminate those which are alike in many respects but with differences that make a difference.

---

[4] B. F. Skinner, *Verbal Behavior* (New York, Appleton-Century-Crofts, 1957). See also B. F. Skinner, "The Programming of Verbal Knowledge," in Eugene H. Galanter, ed., *Automatic Teaching: The State of the Art* (New York, John Wiley & Sons, Inc., 1959), and B. F. Skinner, "The Science of Learning and the Art of Teaching," and others, in A. A. Lumsdaine and Robert Glasser, eds., *Teaching Machines and Programmed Learning* (Washington, Department of Audio-Visual Instruction, National Education Association, 1960), also, the list of Skinner's publications, Lumsdaine and Glaser, *op. cit.,* p. 715.

For example, the letter *M* may be written or printed in many ways, in upper or lower case, in script, or different sizes and kinds of type face, but it is still an *M*. So may the letter *N*. But the only *significant* difference is the second loop. Likewise language sounds, arithmetic symbols, characteristics of biological species, machine parts, art objects, and the like must be discriminated. Sometimes the same stimulus means different things in different patterns, whether it is a dot, a word, a tone, or a disease symptom. Professional training consists partly in an increasing ability to discriminate small differences which the untrained person does not see. To develop competence of this kind, instruction is necessary. The instructor reduces the extent of the field of stimuli, filters out the irrelevant with his instructions, and in various ways points to the significant differences, contrasting the patterns which are similar yet different. For this purpose, various audiovisual devices are extremely helpful and often vitally necessary.

Mediating Conditions

In any environment there are many stimuli that are likely to effect the response. These are of different kinds. One kind can be called concomitant variations, like the instructions or the different kinds of *M's* and *N's,* or the different shapes, colors, sizes, and the like, of objects that are nevertheless classified together and are to be responded to in the same way, *if* the variations do not make a difference. Another group includes the conditions under which the response is to be made— the group atmosphere, depending on the people present, the remarks they make whether encouraging or discouraging, or other distractions. These mediating conditions, as they are called, are stimuli which act upon the learner before he makes his response, sometimes even before he shows up at all, as evidenced by his expectancies, his anxiety or enthusiasm about the prospect. As attitudes they become intervening variables derived not only from his previous mental state but also from his responses, and may be positive or negative with respect to any aspect of the situation. These factors, together with the instructions and the demands of the situation, likewise affect the nature of the response to the perceived stimuli. Instructions, if verbalized, follow the formula, "When you see that, do this." Carried in memory, such directions provide a readiness or set. Some responses that might be made are shunted off on a side track, as it were, in favor of those which are required by the situation, and the set continues to determine the nature of the sequential behavior. Many of the mediating conditions are subject to the control of the school personnel, who are responsible for managing the environment. But the set-up of the conventional classroom frequently makes it very difficult to optimize these conditions.

Response Out-put

What the learner does depends largely on the environmental stimuli or in-put. If the in-put is perfectly controlled, the response may be well-nigh perfect. For example, in classical conditioning if a learner can already make a certain response to stimulus A, he can be conditioned to make the same response to a substitute stimulus B by repeatedly making the response to the two together. A great deal of learning is of this kind: learning to respond to words when one can already make the same response to the objects the words represent, as when a child says "tree" when he sees the letters TREE, if he could previously say "tree" when he saw one. Concept enlargement (stimulus generalization) is a similar process in which one learns to classify objects with a multitude of concomitant variations under the same name, whether it is to recognize, for example, that oaks and evergreens are both trees, or to recognize the different kinds of oaks. The process is the same for more abstract concepts such as incandescence, phoneme, or compromise. Here it will be recognized that not only audiovisual materials but also programmed lessons can take over.

The situation is somewhat different when the learner is unable to make the necessary response—pronounce the word, sound the trumpet, operate a computer, or solve a mathematical problem. In such cases, the instructor can emphasize the cues to which the learner should attend, give specific verbal directions, and demonstrate right and wrong ways so as to reduce sharply the number of wrong responses. The learner can thus make an approximation which progressively improves with successive trials until the correct response is made, and with further practice habituated.

Feedback

Such progress is impossible, however, without what is referred to as feedback, which means a report on the results of the trial, the degree of success of the response in attaining the goal. If a beginner shoots a gun at a tin can on a fence post and misses, he doesn't know whether he fired too high, too low, or too wide, so he cannot be expected to improve. Experiments have shown that without a knowledge of results there is no tendency for the most frequent responses to canalize and become still more frequent except as they become simpler and easier, which does not necessarily mean that they become more nearly correct. There are various ways in which a knowledge of results can be obtained by the learner. Sometimes he can see them well enough himself, or hear them, or feel them kinesthetically, as in motor skills. In others, the instructor can augment the feedback, particularly if the learner has no means of knowing the results, by saying, "Right" or "Wrong." Or he can make it possible for the learner to compare the product with the correct response as in programmed learning, or record the time of the performance, measure the distance, or show the learner his performance in a mirror, on a film, or as recorded on tape.

In addition to knowledge of results the feedback may include an explanation of why things went wrong and verbal directions for modifying the response: "Look, here's what you did. Now try to do it *this* way!" Also it may be the occasion for new information for which the learner was not previously ready, but which is now needed as an explanation of some of the finer points, or as a pointer to what to do next.

Reinforcement

Psychologists and educators talked of reward and punishment until Pavlov's term, *reinforcement,* came into general use. Animal experimenters usually used food and shock, Thorndike in his experiments on human subjects employed the words, *right* and *wrong*—knowledge of results without further affective accompaniments. Schools in general have depended on punishments more than on rewards to keep the lamp of learning bright. One old-time schoolmaster who should have been an accountant kept a meticulous record of the hundreds of punishments he had inflicted by cane, rod, ruler, and hand, boxes on the ear, and slaps over the mouth and head. One wonders how he was able to decide which weapon he would use from his arsenal. Yet only recently the Research Division of the National Education Association reported a survey revealing that 72 per cent of the elementary and 58 per cent of the secondary teachers favored the use of corporal punishment. Again, one wonders, this time about the value of that highly praised personal contact of teachers and pupils. The effect of punishment, an aversive stimulus, is not merely that of teaching avoidance of a specific response, which it often fails to do for the reason that learners are apt to forget which response was punished, and if they do, they may not care. It also tends to produce anxiety or an antagonistic attitude toward the entire learning situation. It has been found that reward, or positive reinforcement, tends to create favorable attitudes and increase the probability that the reinforced response will be remembered and repeated when the situation recurs. For animals, particularly rats and pigeons, schedules of reinforcement have been worked out according to which the effectiveness of various frequencies has been determined. Similarly for human learners, it is not necessary to reinforce a response each time it is made, but it is necessary that the reinforcement be considered as a reward by the learner. A pupil may not respond favorably to too many "Very goods."

Reinforcement apparently has three effects which the able tutor employs: (1) to motivate continued activity ("You are doing much better, making real progress."); (2) to fix the response regularly reinforced so that it is more likely to recur ("That's right, that's just it; now do it again the same way."); (3) to bring about improvement by reinforcing the response that is most nearly correct ("That's better, you almost had it that time."). But in classes such individual attention to all the successive steps of learning for all the pupils is impossible. As a consequence correct responses are often not reinforced, or perhaps by mistake the wrong ones are, and learning is slow and inefficient. Teaching machines can be of real help at this point.

Of course a teacher is not the only source of reinforcement. It may come from other pupils, although sporadically and sometimes incorrectly. Or it may come from the learner himself when he recognizes that his response is correct or nearly so. No one knows exactly what the mechanism of reinforcement actually is. Thorndike referred to it as the "confirming" ("O.K." or "yes") reaction made *by the learner* when he more or less consciously realizes either from external sources or from his own knowledge, as in reading or studying, that his response is correct. It should be added that the learner may think he is correct when he is not and so confirm wrong responses, which points to the need for instruction. Otherwise, as has been said, people will know a great many things that are not so.

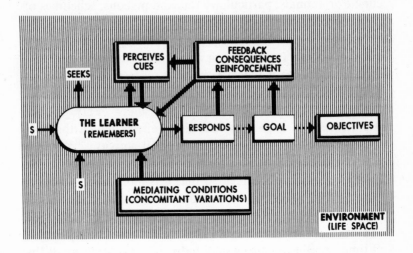

FIGURE 2. The Organism Learns. Learning experiences are here attached to the diagram of the dynamic organism as it appeared in Figure 1. The important mediating conditions affect the learner's response. The *feedback,* in the form of *reinforcement* and other *consequences,* becomes a part of the newly perceived stimulus situation containing additional *cues* to which the next and succeeding responses are made, though somewhat different ones from the first and presumably somewhat improved. The process is repeated in successive trials with closer and closer approximations to the goal of perfection sought. The goal may be an intermediate one serving as a means to the later attainment of other goals which constitute the wider *objectives* of learning.

THE TRADITIONAL SCHOOL ENVIRONMENT

On the basis of this brief view of the learner as a dynamic organism, and of the influence of the controlled environment on learning, it is now possible to evaluate the traditional methods of instruction and their effectiveness in helping children of widely differing abilities.

The Classroom

The familiar administrative unit is *"the* classroom." Children and young people are grouped according to grades, a thirteen-year span from *K* through 12. *"The* teacher" is in charge of each classroom and is expected to control the pupils in it, teach them, test them, grade them, and finally to send them, or most of them, on to the teacher in another classroom. All this goes on behind closed doors. Occasionally there are visitors who may or may not see what is typical. The profession has consistently opposed basing pay increases on the observed quality of classroom performance. In no other occupation except in restricted areas of military operations is the same secrecy preserved.

The development of this generally accepted unit reached its apogee in the so-called self-contained classroom. The teacher and his wards are virtually locked in, and although an occasional art or music teacher is admitted to provide specialized instruction, this is done only under the eye of the regular teacher who is expected to be competent, at least at the elementary level, to handle adequately all branches of instruction and manage the learning environment for thirty to forty or more children.

But whether self-contained or not, the teacher-class situation is taken for granted. Few even pause to ask what a grade (or class) actually is. Supposedly a group of young people equally prepared for the same instruction, it is actually a heterogeneous collection of children of widely differing abilities, usually as many as there are seats for, who are of about the same age and who happen to live in the same neighborhood.

How It Works

We might do well to take a candid look at a more or less typical class in some subject, say, at the junior high level to see how present-day educational theory actually works in practice. We can then compare what we observe with what might be. The building may have been built in the late 1800's, brick, with narrow windows and a square tower in front for the school bell, and very little playground. It may be of the resplendent piano-box variety popular in the 1920's, limestone trim with large windows, wide hallways, and long staircases. Or it may be a modern structure of glass and tile, all on one floor. It doesn't make much difference which class we visit, for although some are better than others, with the exception of the gymnasium and shop they are all much alike. The principal greets us cordially and after exchanging a few remarks, we are ushered into a room more or less at random.

The teacher is talking and some of the students seem to be listening, but others are paying little attention. Two are reading paperbacks behind their textbooks, three are gazing out the window. One handsome youngster is surreptitiously slipping a note to one of the girls who smiles, blushes, and nods to him. Two are whispering eagerly together, and a third is trying to get in on the conversation. The teacher becomes aware of the disturbance, interrupts the explanation, accompanied by some rather confusing marks on the chalkboard, faces the class, and in a different but not unkind tone tells them they should pay attention, that this is important and they will be held responsible for it on the next examination. The class comes to order—that is, all face the front looking innocent and charming. Obviously they like their teacher, but desirable as this is, they did not come to school to learn to like teachers. The explanation is concluded and followed by questions. One student's answer reveals complete ignorance of what he is talking about, and a half a dozen hands shoot up. The student who is called on makes the correction. "Old Faithful," a lad near us mutters. The teacher looks in his direction but unperturbed asks how many understand. The same half dozen hands reappear. So the teacher starts again, this time dropping back to a simpler level of discourse. The readers, window-watchers, and whisperers return to their former occupations, and the hand-wavers slump in their seats with a sigh, or at least they seem to, although we may be only imagining it. The explanation now is labored and, let's face it, dull, though sincere and earnest. It is not quite clear what its relation is to the previous explanation. The teacher's voice gradually becomes a little louder in order to be heard above the increasing though subdued noise from the class members who, with an eye on the clock, are shuffling papers, closing books and getting out others. For when the bell rings they will have to be motivated by the next subject.

Between classes we thank the teacher and make a few polite and appreciative noises. We get the impression that it would have been better if we had not appeared that day, as the teacher remarks that this is a rather difficult group: "They are all nice kids, but some are definitely retarded and others are not working up to capacity. But that boy that made the correction—he has real ability."

Certainly this classroom was not so bad as some nor so good as many others; the surroundings were pleasant, the "live" teacher was dedicated to the task at hand. Feedback came from the class as to how they were receiving the instruction, the few who "recited" were rewarded when they gave the right answers and corrected and encouraged when they did not. Seemingly the system was perfect, but somehow, as so often happens, things didn't click. There must be some reasons. Here in the average classroom is the glory and the tragedy of the American schools—and of many others—opportunity for all, realized by only a few, where the bright *can* learn what they are expected to and the others—well, they probably learn something.

It is hardly necessary to provide a picture of classrooms which are better or worse, though a few details might be mentioned. With really poor instruction the pupils are likely to be antagonistic. Funny noises are heard which the teacher cannot locate and missiles of various sorts occasionally fly through the air—paper darts, chalk, or erasers. The teacher glares, scolds, or threatens, and sends some children from the room. He is likely to be weak in knowledge of his subject matter, and for this and possibly for grammatical errors in his speech, he may be a subject of ill-disguised ridicule. He hears recitations to which class members pay little or no attention, and to them his explanations are just so much talk. Variety is lacking as is any opportunity for enjoyment or creativity. No one learns very much.

At the other extreme we have the so-called gifted teachers; fortunately there are probably a great many with varying degrees of giftedness, and descriptions vary. Of course, the popular, well-liked teacher has an advantage even though his instruction may be chaotic. He probably talks much less than the poor teacher, and the pupils not only answer questions but ask them, and are likely to quash any incipient disturbance themselves. The class may be engaged in a single project, or small group projects. Or the teacher may be instructing one group while two or three other groups are working, either individually or under the direction of a group leader. This and other schemes are employed in order to adapt as much as possible to the differences in pupil abilities. But even for the gifted teacher it is a well-nigh hopeless task to adequately encourage, explain, demonstrate, discuss, drill, correct, and reward—with the wide range of abilities in the classroom.

The futility is dramatically revealed in the evaluation procedure, which is the same whether the instruction is good, bad, or indifferent. Written examinations will be administered and perhaps a half dozen or so pupils will obtain the top mark; the others will be distributed below them roughly following the bell-shaped curve euphemistically called "normal," but ironically indicating varying degrees of ignorance. The majority have no hope of success, but they will "pass," a strangely meaningless word except at the end of the year. Actually they are not expected to know what they were "taught." The tests are designed so as to reveal this expectation; there would be something the matter with the testing procedure if all the students got the same high score indicating that they had learned what they had been taught. The presumption is that much of what the students are supposed to learn is actually regarded as useless, since they "pass" whether they learn it or not. Besides, no one really knows what any child has learned and what he has not—only that he makes a certain score on tests and answers questions in a way that the teacher thinks is good, average, or poor in relation to the other children in the class. Surely it is possible to do better than this.

The Method of Marking

The method of marking commonly employed can well be examined instead of being taken for granted. The teacher usually gives all the students much the same work to do since they are in the same room, and evaluates their work according to the average achievement of the group, which is called a norm. Some below the norm are said to be unable to do the work of that grade, which only means they have not learned to do as well as the average of that grade. Occasionally teachers have been told that they should bring the laggards up to the norm, though this particular bit of professional ignorance is not as common as it was in the earlier days of testing. Now the pressure is on those who for various and sometimes obvious reasons are not "working up to capacity." The situation is not much improved by finding the achievement averages of a number of such grades and calling them national norms.

At best, the marking system assumes that the majority in the grade or class are incompetent (below A), but gives no inkling as to which pupils are incompetent in what. With carefully prepared programming there is no reason that each pupil could not really learn what is needed if it is within the limits of his competence. Specific learning objectives that are worthy of being met can be. Perhaps only a few students need to be competent in performances in which more students could be, and perhaps unknown areas of ignorance are desired or at least harmless. It seems reasonable to suppose, however, that the schools should know what they are teaching and what they are not—and why.

Referring to laboratory experiments, B. F. Skinner is reported to have said that "the animal is always right"; if he doesn't learn what he was expected to, the fault lies with the experimenter. Similarly, it might be added that if a student "fails" or does not learn what he is taught, either such content might as well be omitted (the expectations are unjustified and he has been classified wrongly), or the technique of instruction is badly designed or otherwise unsatisfactory.

If the mythical man from Mars should examine this situation, he might ask some embarrassing questions. He might ask why pupil X and pupil Y should both be in the fifth grade when X is maturing so slowly that he is actually at the second-grade level, while Y is such a fast grower that he is achieving at the eighth-grade level. When the teacher explains about the normal probability curve, in his innocence the Martian asks if pupils of different ability are taught together in order to make a curve. And while the teacher is thinking that one over, the thought occurs to the Martian that the curves for different grades must overlap, and he asks why the people at the same level of ability are taught separately. The teacher knows the answer to that one: it is better to keep together in the same class those who are in about the same age group. The Martian asks why. But before he gets the answer he notes that there are scores and marks and asks what the difference is. Glad to be off the hook, the teacher points out that marks are subjective judgments the teacher makes, taking everything into consideration—a kind of general estimate of the student's ability. "And what of the reliability and validity that are so important for scores?" the Martian asks, but he realizes he has outstayed his welcome and flits back home to report that Earth is certainly a queer place, a bit on the irrational side with little that would be of more than archeological interest.

Why Group Instruction?

Marking methods are largely the consequence of the classroom organization with its annual promotions, a pattern of procedure which is generally assumed to be necessary. The original purpose of the system of grouping children in grades and classes is obvious enough—to enable one teacher to instruct several persons at the same time instead of tutoring them individually. It came about by following the easiest way, an administrative convenience. With a six- or seven-year range of ability in a grade, the purpose is not satisfactorily served, but the grade remains. In order to improve the situation, teachers are told to divide the children in the grade rooms or classes into smaller groups of equivalent ability. This is a bit tricky, but docile teachers, believing like their superior officers that the grade system is necessary, try it anyway in spite of all the disadvantages. And strangely enough the system works fairly well, for children do "seek" and conform, and some learn quite a bit. No doubt much that they have failed to learn never will be missed. And there is the added advantage of pupil interaction, discussion, and planning, in short, learning to work with others. Although it is not always found, this kind of experience should be provided for, but it is not the only educational objective. By way of contrast, group instruction often actually interferes with learning because of mediating conditions—distractions due to misbehavior, embarrassment to the bright pupils in being right and to dull pupils in being wrong, inability of the teacher to give undivided attention, and so on. It is not necessary to assume that grouping by grades is a given, a must for all instruction.

Administrative Devices

Many means have been employed to correct for the disadvantages of group instruction, for example, by changing promotion policies, which vary widely in different schools. Pupils who would be failed in one town pass in another. Since it has been found that most pupils do better in the next grade than those of equivalent ability do by repeating a grade, some schools pass everybody, the euphemistic name for which is social promotion, a procedure that has drawn the fire of those who opine that a pupil should not be rewarded for what he has not succeeded in doing. Such critics are guilty of two errors. One is that they mistake promotion for a reward instead of a method of classification, and the other is that they think there are objective standards of achievement for each grade instead of subjective marking procedures. Double promotions are the simplest for brighter students who, oddly enough, do not seem to suffer from skipping a year's instruction.

A number of schemes for homogeneous grouping have been used. Double-track systems have been tried, but they are administratively difficult. Children are placed in $x, y,$ and z groupings of the bright, average, and dull, but borderline cases, social class, and the methods of marking present difficulties. Special classes have been set up for the mentally handicapped, and for the superior, which for some strange reason some have thought to be undemocratic. More recently, particularly in high schools, classes have been formed on the basis of subject-matter competence, so that a student might be in an advanced class in one subject and in an average class in another. This is a definite step forward and could well be employed as a transitional device toward a more effective means of adaptation to individual differences.

Similarly, the ungraded room [5] is another valuable innovation, particularly for the first three grades, where length of stay, whether two years or six, depends largely on the development of reading ability. When a pupil is sufficiently good at reading to use it as a tool to learn about other subjects, he goes on to the fourth-grade group. Instead of assuming the universal necessity of traditional grades and classes, educators might well ask what other possibilities there are. Individualized instruction has been tried, and popularized under the Dalton and Winnetka plans. But it was found difficult to produce adequate teaching materials, the grade concept which was maintained reaffirmed the old difficulties, and the administrative machinery fell of its own weight. The results simply did not seem worth the effort.

Now that programming for teaching machines is developing, however, it might be well to take another look at the possibilities. With programmed instruction, as will be explained later, arbitrary grouping is no longer necessary. Pupils can proceed at their own rate. Those who are together in a particular subject, whatever their age or "grade," can meet together for testing, appropriate discussions, and film or television showings.

THE TEACHER-MANAGED ENVIRONMENT

It is not difficult to see why these administrative efforts to adapt learning to the student differences in grade and class have been something less than successful. Teaching requires the control and management of the learner's environment. By what he says and writes and does, a teacher presents stimuli and modifies learner responses in the direction of the accepted immediate goals and more remote objectives of education. What kinds of things is a teacher expected to do in

[5] See John I. Goodlad and Robert H. Anderson, *The Nongraded Elementary School* (New York, Harcourt, Brace & World, Inc., 1959).

order to control and manage the environment? What are the roles of a teacher?

These roles are so familiar that to list them may seem quite unnecessary. But changes have crept up so gradually that people do not generally realize what a heterogeneous and actually impossible array of activities "the teacher" is expected to perform.

Early Teacher Roles

A century or more ago in Europe and in America, the tasks were simple. The schoolmaster was janitor, disciplinarian, technician, and bookholder. As janitor or custodian he swept out the one-room school building and kept the fire going in the stove. As disciplinarian, he applied the switch, birch rod, or other aversive stimuli to pupils who did not recite or behave as well as he thought they should. In many rural schools, the incoming schoolmaster had to fight the biggest boy in school, and remained on the job only if he won out. As technician, he had to keep his switches in good working order, and make the quill pens for those far enough advanced to be able to use them. He held the book for spelling and other lessons and set the model for penmanship. It was a simple life but a rough one, a career followed by many disreputable characters, and also by many fine young men including some future professors who earned a little money teaching school to give them their start in college.

Present-Day Teacher Roles

With the coming of vast numbers of children into the schools, the increasing complexity of Western civilization, and the advent of new knowledge and new philosophical and scientific theories of education, all this began to change. Now the teacher's roles are beyond anything that would have been dreamed of in the earlier simpler days. These roles may be listed briefly as follows:

Custodian: water plants, care for animals, clean blackboards, take care of books and equipment, and do a bit of dusting, and general housekeeping.

Clerk: collect money for school events, sell milk, fill out attendance sheets, keep records—academic, health, and other—do mimeographing, and order supplies.

Foster-parent: suspect and refer health problems, provide first aid; serve as nursemaid for smaller children, giving help with overshoes and other clothing; provide younger children with "tender loving care" and older children with security, warmth, and affection.

Disciplinarian: do police duty in the classroom, corridors, lunchroom, and playground, and detective work to discover offenders; serve as judge, jury, and chief executioner in bringing miscreants to justice.

Examiner: select, construct, administer, and score informal and standardized tests, evaluate achievement and rate character for report cards, decide on the failure or promotion of pupils.

Audio-visualist and technician: make charts and chalkboard drawings, put up wall decorations and displays, and select, locate, transport, and operate projection equipment.

Librarian: contribute to the selection of texts, readings, and documents, fetch books from the library, and sometimes maintain a small library in the classroom.

Student adviser: help students in planning their academic programs.

Therapist: counsel with students and with their parents and help them with their adjustment problems.

Recreation leader: sponsor hobby clubs, social and athletic events, and other school activities.

Responsible citizen: take part in parent-teacher meetings and in local church and social work; be an intelligent voter. (Some enthusiasts have suggested that teachers should enter politics!)

But this list includes no teaching, so the following as a minimum should be added:

Communicate with pupils having a wide range of mental ability.

Plan and prepare lessons and develop instructional materials.

Assess readiness for instruction.

Demonstrate equipment, skills, and processes.

Give out information.

Explain facts and their relationships leading to the development of concepts and generalizations.

Provide educational feedback, reinforce and motivate student efforts.

Lead discussions so as to arouse questions and develop original thinking and creativity. And for a proper background, keep up with the professional and content literature, and conduct research.

There is no question but that all these tasks and more should be carried on by properly qualified school personnel. But it is no discredit to the profession to say that to expect that they can all be handled competently by one person is to expect what never was and never will be. In the current engineering language, not even the best teachers behave in optimum fashion. They do not and cannot have sufficient knowledge of the output required with the tolerance limits, of the input variables, or of the work objects and techniques that might be used. A psychologist has opined that it will be necessary somehow to change teacher behavior, and a philosopher has gone him one better by writing, that "the point in bringing about a significant reconstruction of education . . . is to reconstruct the teacher."

Instead of trying to force these divergent roles on all teachers, whatever their varied aptitudes, skills, and interests, it might be wiser to change the jobs, to reduce the roles, in other words, to reconstruct the school organization. Specialization along the lines of particular interests and talents would assure not only greater proficiency but also greater satisfaction. The advent of teaching machines, television, and other innovations provides the occasion for a reorganization of the various responsibilities of the teaching personnel in the interest of greater efficiency and effectiveness. This cannot be brought about by administrative fiat, but rather by cooperative planning by teachers and administration.

FLEXIBILITY

Many of the difficulties besetting educators seeking to meet the problems presented by student differences tend to fall away when the idea of the teacher-classroom organization is abandoned, and the possibilities of greater flexibility are recognized. This flexibility is to be noted particularly in class and room size, in staff utilization, and in flexible scheduling.[6]

Class and Room Size

While the plan of having twenty-five to thirty students to a room may seem to be the ideal arrangement under present conditions, from the various experiments with different-sized class groups it may be concluded that this arrangement is actually the least satisfactory—too small to be efficient, and too large to permit adequate instruction. Instead, a combination of large classes, say of 90 to 175 students, and small classes of about 15, supplemented by arrangements for individual study seems to be the present trend, with a ratio in per cent of a student's time of about 40-20-40 respectively. Decisions as to the use of each will be made not on the basis of subject matter being taught but of method employed and objectives sought.

Much of what a teacher says and does is just as effective before a large group as a smaller one, so it would seem un-

[6] See "And No Bells Ring," 57-minute film on large-group instruction, small-group discussion, independent study, and the teacher team. National Association of Secondary School Principals, 1201 Sixteenth St., N.W., Washington, D.C. (1961).

necessary to repeat it several times to smaller groups. Under this head would come the giving of information and instructions, orientation sessions, explanations, and demonstrations. For example, if a physics teacher has four sections, one lecture-demonstration a week to the combined sections leaves him three extra periods—more time to prepare a really good lecture with demonstration materials, or time for individual or small-group conferences with his students. Such large groups can be brought together to introduce new material, to motivate and inspire the students (the speaker must be good!), to explain difficult points, to explore new territory, and to furnish enrichment beyond the usual demands of the course. An "outside speaker" is as a rule much more satisfied to speak to a large group. Films, musical and dramatic events, and any other occasions when the class is an audience, and there are many of them, lend themselves to large-group presentation. It is not necessary to wait for team teaching to experiment with large classes.

The small group is advocated on the principle that learning takes place through personal interaction of students and teachers. A face-to-face group of twelve to fifteen is considered optimum for discussion, preferably around a table. This size permits all participants to have their say, to ask and answer questions about what has been presented to the large group, about their individual progress perhaps on programmed material, or other matters. Small group gatherings can be used for helping students with special projects, for co-curricular activities, resource presentations, review and coaching sessions, listening to recordings, musical ensemble or foreign language practice, and so on. Like a seminar, the small group provides the opportunity for experience in critical thinking and creativity, or like a committee, for group planning and group decision-making.

The phrase, individual study, seems to be replacing homework and seatwork, but the difference is in more than the name. While some individual study can be programmed, and much of it no doubt, should provide practice on what has been learned, some of it should be exploratory—outside reading and some creative writing, composing, or other art work. No sonnet or symphony was every written by a committee, and the plans put forward by committee action are usually what some one of the members previously worked out and presented for its consideration. In schools it is possible to overemphasize the importance of the group.

Flexibility in class size naturally calls for flexibility in room size. The school architects therefore are now turning away from the "egg crate" type of construction, with all rooms about the same size except for the auditorium, cafeteria, and gymnasium or combinations thereof. Large rooms, some divided by retractable partitions, conference rooms, and carrels or booths for independent study areas are appearing on the drawing boards and taking shape in brick and mortar.

Staff Utilization

The introduction of teacher aides and team teaching constitutes a further illustration of developing flexibility in the modern school. The Bay City, Michigan, plan for employing teacher aides grew out of the discovery that a large per cent of a teacher's time is taken up with nonprofessional activities that could be performed quite as well by less highly trained persons. A glance at the list of teacher roles above bears out this conclusion. With proper assistance teachers might do either a better job of teaching or as good a job with larger classes. One might as well expect a surgeon to spend time preparing the patient for an operation or rolling bandages as expect a teacher to play all the supporting educational roles.

Three sources for assistance have been considered—clerks, trainees, and competent lay people. There is no unanimity in the decision as to just what their tasks should be, but the following trends have been noted: clerks for keeping accounts and records, typing and mimeographing, etc.; assistants for libraries and shops and for conducting field trips; supervisors for halls, playgrounds, study halls, and shops; and lay readers for grading tests and other papers, and such tasks as helping pupils make up work and orienting new pupils who arrive in the middle of the term. It can be seen at once that questions would be raised as to the competence of uncertified personnel for one or another of these tasks, particularly that of the lay reader. Further, the plan unnecessarily presupposes the conventional classroom. It may, perhaps, be regarded as a transitional stage, an initial attempt to modify current methods of staff utilization that will be taken care of in a more satisfactory fashion with the development of the systems approach of modern technology (to be described later).

One of the most dramatic of recent innovations in staff utilization is what is called team teaching.[7] In general it is an administrative arrangement whereby anywhere from two to six or so teachers are in charge of a group of perhaps 75 to 250 students. The plan takes various forms. Most common is the one with two or more teachers with varying skills or levels of competence under a team leader who is a more highly paid, experienced teacher, and who is responsible for the operation. Sometimes the leadership is "situational" in a cooperating group in one or more subjects. Sometimes the team is a pair, e.g., a master teacher and beginning teacher in the same subject.

Some think it better to have different subject-matter specialists serve as a team for two or three grades in the belief that continuity and competence are thus increased, others, that a team should serve pupils in the same grade. Still others believe that with the individual progress permitted by pro-

[7] See Robert Boguslaw and Elias H. Porter in Gagné, *op. cit.,* pp. 386–416; also, National Association of Secondary School Principals, *Locus on Change—Staff Utilization Studies,* National Education Association Bull. Vol. 46, No. 270 (January, 1962).

grammed learning, different staff teams will form spontane-
ously. Whatever plan is followed, it will provide opportunity
for leadership, which should attract superior individuals to
teaching if the salary is commensurate with the responsibility.
The plan is aimed in part at adapting to individual differences,
since large groups can be broken down into smaller groups
to be handled by different team members for special purposes.
But other advantages are claimed for it. The whole group can
be easily brought together as a large class from time to time
for matters of general interest or concern. It breaks up the
self-contained classroom and permits teachers to plan together, to handle the subject matter in which they are competent, to work with students they are better able to get along
with, to substitute for each other temporarily or brief the substitute teacher, and to reduce the distractions by carrying on
while one of them takes care of a localized disturbance.

The advantages claimed for team teaching have been summarized as follows: [8] It

> adapts to teacher differences, making use of the peculiar skill
> and talent of individual teachers, so pupils get better teaching,
> adapts to student differences, permitting more work with in-
> dividuals and small groups,
> provides diversity of experience for students, who thus have
> more than one teacher,
> provides for the economy of larger classes,
> permits flexible subgrouping within the larger class, with a
> separate teacher for each subgroup,
> gives teachers time for preparation and planning and more
> professional activities, and
> provides an internship for trainees and an apprenticeship for
> beginners.

It is an anomaly that there is now no differentiation of
teaching responsibility, no real career opportunity. The in-

[8] Luvern C. Cunningham, "Team Teaching: Where Do We Stand?"
Administrator's Notebook, Vol. 8, No. 8 (April, 1960).

experienced teacher is now expected to do all the things an experienced teacher does. There is no chance to work up in the profession, and apart from receiving arbitrary pay increases for length of service or for postgraduate credit, promotion can come only by moving into administrative positions or by leaving the profession.

Where team teaching has been tried, it has worked very well. As a rule, teachers are enthusiastic about it, partly no doubt because they no longer work in isolation as members of what has been called "the lonely profession," and can spend more time in the company of their peers. Younger pupils have not missed the single father or mother figure, academic achievement has been at least as good as with the conventional class organization, and the satisfaction of pupils has been high.

Where difficulties have arisen it has sometimes been the result of inadequate planning, and sometimes the inability of some team member to cooperate or carry his share of the load. Wanda Mitchell [9] has noted that it is often difficult for a teacher to give up the classroom where his word is law, his method the right and only one, and his decision final. With team teaching, compromise is necessary. No successful team can have two leaders. Differences of opinion may arise on how to divide the tasks, and the hierarchy that forms may cause conflicts, or there may be jealousy on the part of those who work only with the smaller groups and therefore have no opportunity to enjoy the glamor of appearing before the large classes.

A number of questions still await satisfactory answers. Perhaps most annoying to the enthusiasts is the question, Why bother with team teaching at all if the work of the learners is no better than under conventional procedures? Although this can be answered on the basis of other advantages, there still

[9] National Association of Secondary School Principals, *op. cit.*, Chap. 23.

seems to be no clear-cut statement of objectives. Whether the method really does deal with individual student differences more satisfactorily than conventional methods is a second question. It seems to have possibilities which have not been fully exploited, especially if programmed learning were included. A third question is, What should be taught in this way? This is largely a question of class size, and the answer depends on what one is trying to do, on the objectives of any particular unit of instruction. A fourth question is one of the roles and competencies of the team members, for nothing approaching a common pattern has emerged. But this may be the source of its greatest strength, that it is sufficiently flexible to adapt itself to different kinds of situations in different kinds of schools.

It is sometimes hard to realize that team teaching and other innovations [10] including the nongraded school and teacher aides, as well as the new media of instruction, are not figments of the imagination, mere impractical dreams. They have actually been put into operation by those who were not satisfied with the *status quo*. But to make such changes in the school organization is not easy. The public, the parents, even many teachers may be satisfied with things as they are. Can one be sure that the proposed changes will actually be better for the students? The nature of planned change [11] has been studied in recent years, and J. Lloyd Trump [12] has described eight ingredients which are briefly outlined below:

1. Experimental studies. Action research is important in determining needs and in evaluating outcomes.

[10] See Arthur D. Morse, *Schools of Tomorrow—Today* (Garden City, Doubleday & Company, Inc., 1960).

[11] Dorwin Cartwright and Alvin Zander, eds., *Group Dynamics Research and Theory*, 2d ed. (New York, Harper & Row, Publishers, 1960); also, Ronald Lippitt and others, *The Dynamics of Planned Change* (New York, Harcourt, Brace & World, Inc., 1958).

[12] "Ingredients of Change," in National Association of Secondary School Principals, *op. cit.*, Chap. 31.

2. Preparing and distributing brochures. The staff and the public must be kept informed, but the documents must be attractive.
3. Speeches by knowledgeable people. Speakers before organized groups, perhaps with slides. But they must be good.
4. Demonstrations by teachers and students. Class demonstrations move too slowly; well-prepared audio-visual programs are better.
5. Using mass media. Newspaper stories, radio and television report what the school has to sell.
6. Issuing summary reports of changes. Reassurance, professionally prepared, with statements by teachers and students should convey a message that will be understood by all.
7. Keeping staff members informed. Those not involved should not feel left out.
8. Encouraging experimental approaches. Change should be planned and pushed by responsible persons.

Flexible Scheduling

The value of a number of common school practices has been questioned—the self-contained classroom, the marking system, grade norms, the promotion system, standard class size, and homogeneous grouping. Perhaps the greatest villain in the piece, however, is the Carnegie unit.[13] This is a device which earlier brought some order out of the chaos of high school courses and facilitated college admissions. Its origin is to be found in the establishment of a fund by Andrew Carnegie for retired college professors. To obtain the grants, so many schools called themselves colleges that the fund was swamped. The trustees therefore set up criteria by which an institution could qualify as a college: its students must have completed

[13] Ellsworth Tompkins and Walter Gaumnitz, *The Carnegie Unit: Its Origin, Status, and Trends,* U. S. Department of Health, Education and Welfare, Bull. 1954, No. 7, 1954; also, Sidney L. Besvinck, "The Expendable Carnegie Unit," *Phi Delta Kappan,* 42 (May, 1961), 356–366.

on entrance a minimum of fourteen standard units of school work. A unit was defined as regular attendance in a course that met one period a day, five days a week, thirty-six weeks a year. This is the Carnegie unit. Scholarship is measured not in terms of quality or quantity of learning, but by sitting-time as shown by the clock and the calendar. Although the plan achieved its purpose and was administratively convenient, the wrong variables were used as criteria. They still are.

The college and university equivalent of the Carnegie unit, the credit hour, is similarly under attack. Some college authorities are doubtful as to whether degrees should be granted solely on the basis of the completion of a specified number of classroom hours and the passing of course examinations. As things are now, time must be spent in class even by students who already have the required proficiency. The adding machine evaluates scholarship: "In any given institution, then, the credit system must be assessed in terms of its relative slavery to blocks of time versus its adequacy in indicating levels of competence. . . . Not only do some educators consider the credit hour an instrument of doubtful validity as a measure of accomplishment of students who come from highly diverse backgrounds; they consider its strictly class-hour interpretation an actual impediment to improvements in teaching-learning patterns.[14]

Carter [15] has written, "Hopefully, the present rigidly compartmentalized class-year system will be broken down in many areas and the student will be allowed to progress at a speed which corresponds to his particular abilities. Children of quite different chronological ages will study material appropriate to their individual abilities, not their age classification." And the same reverse approach was suggested by

[14] Lanora G. Lewis, "The Credit System in Colleges and Universities," U.S. Office of Education, Bul. No. 9, 1961.

[15] Launor F. Carter, "The Challenge of Automation in Education," in Coulson, *op. cit.,* p. 12.

James B. Conant [16] who opened the road leading toward individualized instruction which the new media make possible when he wrote: "We hold the time or duration of a course constant—ordinarily one year—and then expect varying degrees of achievement. . . . One might consider holding the standards constant but varying the time allotted to the study of the subjects."

Continuity

Some students, for example, can complete "a year" of algebra in half that time, while others, if they should take it at all, would need two years. Foreign languages are now being started in the elementary school. A common procedure is for a student to take one language for "two years," then drop it and take another, thus gaining only a smattering of each. Instead, he might better continue with one of them on a reduced schedule of instruction and practice through high school in order to retain and add to what has been learned. Time could also be saved for experience in other subjects so that a choice would not be necessary between shop, art, and music, for example.

The false continuity of successive grades, for which some pupils are not ready and for which others have been ready for a year or two, can and should be replaced by a true continuity. Already some schools have "split-week" courses that do not meet five times a week, and others have periods of differing length—from twenty-two minutes to two hours, and thus permit students to continue in a subject, say, the French they started in elementary school, and to begin each fall where they left off the preceding spring, no matter what "grade" they are in.

New forms of organization make any educational writing about *the* teacher and *the* classroom sound a bit quaint. In-

[16] James B. Conant, "Another Look at the Comprehensive High School," *NEA Journal,* 51 (May, 1962), 29–31.

stead, it is more satisfactory to think about the possibilities of specialized instructional personnel in different-sized school-rooms with the children doing the tasks they can do and at the rate they can do them. There can probably be no single organizational structure that will be best for all schools. But within a set of principles serving as guidelines, adaptations can gradually be made that are acceptable in each local situation.

3

Environmental Control: Technological Change

THE WORK OF THE SCHOOLMASTER was once comparatively simple, but like his rural employers he lacked scientific knowledge and equipment. A rapidly growing technology, however, has produced striking changes both in agriculture and in education. Before discussing what are sometimes referred to as the new media [1] of instruction, it may be profitable to examine and evaluate the old and the current as the means that teachers now have at their disposal for controlling and managing the environment in order to promote learning. The possibilities of combining all available media in a modern educational technology can then be considered.

TRADITIONAL MEDIA

We would not expect any one medium to take the place of all the others, but it is possible that each has certain functions

[1] The word *media* has become accepted usage despite the fact that in recent years auditoria have become auditoriums, curricula curriculums, and a little off beat, phenomena phenomenons. If data should become datums, it might have a better chance of remaining in the plural where, like media, it belongs!

that it can perform most effectively and to the advantage of all concerned. The traditional media are, of course, familiar enough, but it is interesting to consider them from a comparative point of view.

The Spoken Word

The earliest medium of instruction was the spoken word. In homes, churches, and armies, on farms, and in business and industry, as well as in the schools, the older people have *told* the younger what was expected of them. Telling was formalized educationally in the lecture (from *legere,* to read). The medieval scholastics read to the assembled students in the days when there were no printed books and few manuscripts. Now with unlimited textual material professors still lecture, and teachers spend most of the class time in talking. Some of this talk is informative; some, no doubt therapeutic for the teacher, serving to relieve his feelings. No one knows how much of this talk goes unheeded, or how much is understood. Probably every teacher at one time or another has experienced a feeling of futility like the one who concluded a careful exposition by saying, "Now that is clear, whether you understand it or not." Some of the teacher's talk is corrective, providing feedback on pupil responses. Whether this is negative or positive and rewarding, as Skinner has said, as a mere reinforcing mechanism, the teacher is out of date.

Children like teachers who are able to "explain things," but it is difficult to do this to the satisfaction of all in a class made of pupils of widely differing abilities. A tutor has the advantage, for he can address himself to the responses of one individual, give specific directions, receive and supply feedback, reduce the number of trials, and so speed up and enrich learning. But even here, no one knows how well these tasks are performed. Demonstrations usually need a vocal accompaniment, and certainly there is no good reason to dispense with the competent discussion leader. On the other hand, pupils in the self-contained classroom may get a little tired of the same voice all day long, referred to by those who are opposed to the developing technology as "the living voice of the teacher," and sometimes as "the voice of the living teacher." While the spoken word will necessarily be an important medium of instruction, many teachers are glad for an occasional respite during which they can turn the responsibility over to some other medium.

The Written Word

Already the use of handwriting for instructional purposes has largely disappeared. Illuminated manuscripts are museum pieces, and the teacher no longer has to set the model for the writing lesson. About all that is left is to present outlines, directions, regulations, and the like, on the chalkboard. Even in teacher-pupil planning, one of the pupils is usually designated as the recorder. Sometimes teachers "correct" the errors in written work. This provides a feedback, though delayed, and offers an excellent opportunity for individual instruction, although there is usually insufficient time to take advantage of it.

FAMILIAR TECHNOLOGICAL ADVANCES

What can teachers do to promote learning besides talk and write? A number of inventions, now largely taken for granted have already found their way into the pattern of conventional instruction.

Movable Type—the Printed Word

The invention of printing from movable type in the fifteenth century equals the invention of the wheel and of the steam and internal-combustion engines in the magnitude of the resultant social change. The profusion of printed materials has virtually outlawed illiteracy, and has provided an embarrassment of riches for education, and at the same time presented a number of difficulties that have not yet been fully resolved.[2] Textbooks have poured from the presses, but experts differ on the best ways to use them. Teachers read them to their classes, ask questions on them, refer students to them, follow them, reject them, select from them, and combine them in course outlines on mimeographed sheets.

Trade books, fiction or other, are produced, many in textbook format, and are studied at the rate of a few pages a day, assigned for outside reading, placed on open shelves, and sometimes locked in the school library because pupils have been negligent in returning them. In paperback editions they are available at drugstores and supermarkets. Workbooks are used for seat work and homework, and are rejected entirely. School libraries function as storage space, but nowadays more often as resource centers for encyclopedias, magazines, journals, newspapers, pamphlets, and public documents, to supplement instruction. Granting that different subjects and different parts of the same subject may call for different proportions of oral and printed instruction, it is nevertheless time for a careful review of the teacher's role in relation to that of the librarian. Ten million elementary and 150,000 secondary school pupils attend schools that have no central library. The average amount spent per pupil on library books comes to about half the average cost of one book. In some school systems new books are unavailable until late in the term because they have to be stamped and catalogued, while in others the necessary work is done more expeditiously by clerks in the central office before the books are sent out to the schools, thus freeing the school librarian for his proper duties.

Those who fear that television or teaching machines will take the place of reading should be assured that the book is

[2] See O. L. Davis, Jr., "Textbooks and Other Printed Materials," *Review of Educational Research*, 32 (April, 1962), Chap. 2.

here to stay. It is noteworthy that information about the new media is found in printed form, not on screen or program, though the latter may be called in for an assist now and then.[3] More information can be provided more conveniently in book or pamphlet form than in any other. Although after leaving school, people may be taught or trained in specific content by means of the new media, these will not always be available, and so earlier practice should have the learner make frequent and profitable use of printed material. Indeed this is just what has happened in some school experimental situations. Particularly after some screen presentation or discussion, pupils have flocked to the library for materials that have been referred to.

One of the chief advantages of the book [4] over oral instruction is that the pupil can go at his own rate, whereas in oral instruction, the teacher sets the pace, which may be about right for the average, but is likely to be too slow or too fast for others. An instructional materials center, of which the library is a part, is in the blueprints of many new schools.

Typewriter and Offset Processes

After nearly two centuries of experimentation, the typewriter came into common use and subsequently the mimeograph, ditto machine, and various offset processes. These made it possible, at relatively low cost, to prepare print-like copies of course and lecture outlines and other data, to say nothing of examinations.

It is doubtful that as much use is made of these materials as should be. Lecturers often report data collected with great effort and leave the student to get as much in his notes as

[3] For example, W. H. Allen, "Teaching Machines," color, 62 frames (Basic Skill Films, 1355 Inverness Dr., Pasadena, California); also, Teaching Machines, Inc., *Principles of Programmed Learning—Demonstration Course* (New York, TMI—Grolier, 1961).

[4] William E. Spaulding, *Look to the School* (New York, The New York Public Library, 1960).

possible for future reference. Slides and filmstrips, to be discussed later, may be used to present such data, but in practice often the fateful, "Next slide please," comes so quickly that the listeners have insufficient time to comprehend what is on the screen, to say nothing of making a record of it. As is often done, a lecturer can present some materials in mimeographed form for later study. Like the screen, duplicated material enables all those in the room to look at the same things at the same time, but only the latter permits later review.

Camera—the Picture

Since Comenius in the seventeenth century published the first school picturebook, illustrations have played an increasingly important part in instruction. From the crude drawings of *Orbis Pictus* and the *New England Primer* and the woodcuts of some early college textbooks we have come a long way to the photographs in black and white and in color that we find in today's textbooks. Some do little more than lend attractiveness and charm. Others provide what early educational psychologists referred to as sense training and, later, object teaching. The picture is not only a remarkably able substitute for realities beyond the reach of the school child, it is also a means to aid him in perceiving significant cues so that discriminations are more precise and concepts more quickly and accurately formed.

Projector—the Screen

The "magic lantern," metamorphosed into the projector with slides and film strips, and then the overhead and opaque projectors, provided a most important extension in the use of the photograph, namely group observation and also convenience in storing. Now, instead of handing pictures around to the class or displaying them at the front where those at the back and sides of the room cannot see them, the teacher can flash them on the screen and all may clearly observe and discuss the same item at the same time. It is often easier to talk about something than to demonstrate it, though the latter may be more effective. Many kinds of visual materials besides those mentioned—flannel boards, magnetic chalk boards, maps, globes, charts, graphs, models, mock-ups, cut-aways, exhibits, and simulators—can be used advantageously for demonstration for different purposes.[5]

The motion picture camera added a valuable though sometimes unnecessary component. Motion is of little value in presenting a picture of a mountain, a leaf, a geological formation, or a painting, for example. But to illustrate a storm, a lava flow, a machine, a motor skill, or any process in which movement is the significant stimulus, a still picture is, of course, far less satisfactory. Slow motion or time expansion and time lapse or time compression, like magnification, reveal what cannot be seen otherwise. And the loop film can provide repetition of a model performance for imitation. It is hardly necessary to point out that projection can be of great instructional value in narrowing the response to the significant aspects of the situation and in providing feedback from the pupil's own imperfect efforts, particularly in the motor skills.

Since most films are relatively short, they tend to be used as an adjunct to supplement instruction. Probably as a consequence of the influence of educational television, whole courses, especially in science, supplemented by textbooks and workbooks, have been developed using 160 or so thirty-minute films. Such long series, like television programs, provide skillful instruction, particularly demonstrations and explanations. Estimates [6] suggest that school-owned films are most economical for programming a lesson series provided at least six schools use the set. If fewer, it is cheaper to rent.

[5] See William C. Beal, "Training Programs and Devices," in Gagné, *op. cit.*, pp. 342–384.

[6] See Robert M. Brown, *Review of Educational Research*, 2 (April, 1962), 198; also, Warren F. Seibert, *ibid.*, p. 205.

Thirty or forty schools are a better minimum for television. For closed circuit TV for fewer than four student sections, costs are higher than conventional instruction, but it has an advantage for 150 to 270 students.

Phonograph—the Recording

The invention of the phonograph in the latter part of the nineteenth century did for sounds what printing did for words and the camera for illustrations. It made possible their reproduction, wide diffusion, and convenient storage. First Edison's tinfoil, later his wax cylinder, then the disc and finally, in 1945, tape were used. For individual listening either separate listening booths or earphones are needed. Recordings have come into common educational use to bring the world's great music and drama into the schoolrooms. They provide feedback for training in speech and pronunciation of foreign languages. Connected with slides and filmstrips, they furnish the accompanying explanations of pictures, diagrams, or cartoons, or the directions for mechanical processes. In view of the increasing number of such processes, industrial concerns are finding this method very effective in trade training. It can be used to advantage in schools, particularly for teaching skills in shop, business, home economics, and arts and crafts courses, freeing the teacher to plan, supervise, and encourage, and so to bring the pupils to a higher level of performance.

The sound track, added to the motion picture film in 1935, has resulted in a rich variety of products of high instructional value,[7] although some are apparently constructed with a view to making an appeal to such a wide range of interest and intelligence, that for many their value is questionable. At present, the projectors are still hard to transport, they may be in

[7] Neal E. Miller and others, "Graphic Communication and the Crisis in Education," *Audio-Visual Communication Review,* Vol. 5, No. 3 (1957), 1–120.

use in another part of the building, or out of order, so they have probably not been so widely used as they should be.

Audio-Visual Materials [8]

If there is uncertainty about the role of the book, there is still more uncertainty about the role of film and tape in education. Are they a means of instruction or merely aids or adjuncts to instruction? Basically, they are amplifiers, which extend the range of the human voice, the eye, and ear; or putting it another way, they bring distant sights and sounds into the schoolroom to individuals or any sized group a room will hold. As such, they are or can be a means of instruction just as a textbook is. But books are taken for granted, whereas unfortunately audio-visual materials are often introduced or not, largely at the whim of the teacher.

It would be interesting to speculate as to what would have been the result if film projection had been invented in the fifteenth century and the printing press in the nineteenth. The book would have had a race to overtake the picture and the spoken word. As a matter of fact, this is virtually what has happened where the battle for literacy is being waged, where there are no roads through swamp and jungle, and the culture has jumped from the footpath to the airplane, skipping the oxcart, the horse and buggy, and the automobile. In such places, films flown in by air are presented in the native language which few can read. Perhaps the audio-visual materials should precede the book even though they were invented later. It is possible that we do not make sufficient use of the inventions we already have, nor make the equipment sufficiently accessible. Teachers should not have to run a film projector delivery service or repair shop. Technicians and others could well keep audio-visual materials in good condition and make

[8] Paul R. Wendt and Gordon K. Butts, "Audio-Visual Materials," *Review of Educational Research, op. cit.*

them as available as the books in the library, and in many places they do.

There is probably little the matter with audio-visual programs that a few more dollars and a little ingenuity could not cure. But as things now stand there is considerable dissatisfaction with the situation. A number of surveys [9] and recommendations have noted the following needs:

Better financial support. The $1.50 found to be the average amount spent per unit of average daily attendance was considered less than half what it should be.

More nearly adequate supply of materials

Development of standard cataloging and library procedures

Increased assistance in curriculum planning and classroom use

Statistical records and evaluations of audio-visual operations

Additional housing space and light control facilities

Varying standards for allocations of equipment and floor space in districts differing in population density

Varying loan periods for different kinds of materials

More research on audio-visual education

Strengthening of teacher education in new media utilization

In colleges, although most of the points would apply to the schools as well, resistance to the use of audio-visual materials was attributed to:

Faculty and administration inertia

Unavailability of films, equipment, or operators when needed

Lack of equipped classrooms or other viewing areas

Problems of obtaining the right material when needed

Lack of budget to provide decentralization of certain materials and equipment

Unavailability of appropriate materials

Lack of information about sources

[9] Reported by James W. Brown and John A. Moldstad, "Administration of Instructional Materials," in the *Review of Educational Research, op. cit.*, 199–204.

Limited time of instructors for locating or designing appropriate materials

Lack of technical assistance for preparation of materials

As previously stated, an instructional materials center is the solution many schools are trying.

NEW TECHNOLOGICAL ADVANCES

A primitive technology early introduced the book for the use of the individual, and later audio-visual equipment for the group. Now, via cable and the airwaves, the possibilities of instruction are extended to individuals and groups in different parts of a building and even to different buildings and different localities. And programmed lessons make possible much greater precision and effectiveness in certain kinds of instruction.

Telephone—the Language Laboratory

The transmission of sound, direct or recorded, by wire and cable, made possible by Bell's invention of the telephone in 1876 coupled with more recent electronic devices, opened the way for the language laboratory. Foreign languages, particularly Latin, Greek, and Hebrew, had been taught in America from the earliest days of secondary and higher education. Since no one was expected to speak these languages, phonetics, grammar, composition, reading, and literature were taught. When modern languages were introduced, traditional grammatical methods were followed (derived from the heavily inflected Latin grammar) with translation the objective. The ability to speak and understand the spoken language was rarely sought and still more rarely attained. During World War I it was unpatriotic to know the language of the enemy, native German teachers were suspect and American teachers of German found themselves without students, while the teaching of French became as popular as the limited number of

French teachers permitted. Sanity gradually returned, and during World War II the importance of modern language study was recognized, particularly for the forces that would occupy foreign territory. But for this purpose, translation was not so important as the ability to use the oral language. Relatively few foreign language teachers could do this, and there was no time for the grammatical methods they knew.

Meanwhile the linguists had been studying the structure of language and the native language sounds—which, however, could not be taught satisfactorily by the usual class methods. The country was scoured for native speakers who drilled small groups on the language sounds and expressions, sometimes having the soldier students repeat words and stock sentences individually, a time-consuming method, or in unison, which made individual correction difficult. A few language lessons based on the linguistic studies were recorded for the Army Area and Language programs. On these records, a native speaker would say a key sentence, then there would be a pause to give time for the student to repeat it. Later developments produced the language laboratory on the principle of the juke box, with the recordings of the native speaker centrally stored and the appropriate lessons transmitted through earphones. Teachers (monitors) and those concerned with making programs observe and help the students and correct and improve the programs.

So obvious were the advantages of such a procedure that by 1962, according to a U. S. Office of Education survey, approximately 2500 secondary schools and over 700 colleges and universities were equipped with some kind of language laboratory. The advantage comes, however, not in recording old-fashioned grammar lessons, nor in using recordings as a mere adjunct to regular teaching. The language laboratory makes its greatest contribution when it is used as an integral part of a program in which instruction in hearing and speaking forms the basis for sequential, cumulative, and carefully recycled development of language skills, each small step building directly on the preceding steps.[10]

Materials and activities thus classify into three basic categories: (1) listening only, for aural comprehension and reading readiness; (2) repeating or "echoing," for improving pronunciation and unconsciously memorizing; and (3) "pattern practice," for learning language structure by hearing and replying to brief statements and questions, all in the foreign language, thus habituating the proper forms.

This emphasis on the spoken language, referred to as the audio-lingual approach, is basic to the modern linguistic methods, the rationale for which is in part that it is the first to develop in the life of the child as well as in the history of culture. The consequence of this emphasis is that instruction provides practice in the discrimination and correct production of language sounds (e.g. beet and bit), as well as in intonation and rhythm. Failure in these skills results in the familiar foreign accent or brogue. Another basic characteristic of the modern linguistic approach is the attention given to the structure of the language itself, with special emphasis on the structures that differ from those of the native language. As a consequence, the method of instruction is inductive—gradually arriving at rules by a process of generalization—instead of deductive, the rules being taught first with the expectation that the student will be able to apply them.

The movement to begin instruction in foreign languages earlier than in the usual high school course is rapidly gaining headway, and there is already considerable literature [11] on FLES (foreign languages in the elementary school). Because of the nature of young children, the audio-lingual methods

---

[10] Gustave Mathieu, "Language Laboratories," *Review of Educational Research,* 32 (April, 1962), Chap. 5.

[11] See bibliography by Marjorie C. Johnson and Ilo Remer, *References on Foreign Languages in the Elementary School,* Office of Education Circular No. 495, rev., 1959.

tend to be used. Children who come from these classes have
difficulty when plunged into high school classes where the old-
fashioned, deductive grammatical methods are still in vogue.
For this reason, attention is being given to the problem of
continuity—opportunity for learners to make continuous
progress in the elementary school and high school, and on
into college. Such continuity calls for a designation of proficiency in more specific terms than years of instruction. Tests
to measure proficiency are being devised, but the task is a difficult one. It involves the measurement of competence in both
reception and production of auditory and visual symbols. On
the reception side it includes sound discrimination, control of
grammatical patterns (e.g. word order), recognition vocabulary, and reception of context (or interpretation of meanings).
More briefly, it requires competence in the ability to read and
to understand the spoken language (for which the single word
aud is being tentatively used). For production, the competencies are similar—pronunciation (sounds, intonation,
and rhythm), use of grammatical patterns, speaking vocabulary, and conveying of meanings, that is, the ability to speak
and write. There is some doubt as to the value of any single
proficiency score though a double score (like the measurement of blood pressure) for oral and written language might
be useful. Any combined score of course, raises problems of
weighting of the component items. But any scheme would be
better than the present units in terms of duration of instruction.

There are three parts to the complete language laboratory:
listening stations,[12] reproduction area or control room, and
monitoring area. The listening stations or positions are small
spaces walled up to a height of four feet or so with acoustic
material, and furnished with a chair, table or shelf, earphones, and often a telephone mouthpiece and dialing ap-

[12] These are variously referred to as booths, carrels, stalls, and
cubicles. *Booth* seems to be the preferred nomenclature. *Cubicle* is not
quite appropriate since its etymological meaning is sleeping space.

paratus for automatic remote control. The student may dial
the lesson he is ready for. He listens to the recorded sentences
which he "echoes," or answers questions asked, an oral adaptation of the Skinnerian teaching machine program. He may
do this through a speaking device so that he hears himself
through his earphones, his voice being amplified so that he
hears what he is saying loudly and clearly. His voice may also
be recorded and played back to him for comparison with that
of the native speaker. But this procedure, perhaps because of
the delay involved, seems as yet to be unnecessarily laborious
in view of the results obtained.

The reproduction area is the control room where tapes are
stored and played, with the sound funneled to the appropriate
booths. The listening stations are situated in the laboratory
proper. The monitoring is done either by a teacher moving
from booth to booth, from a monitoring area or console in
the same room, or from a sound-proof room with two-way
telephonic transmission. The monitor may be signaled for
help, or he can tune in on any lesson to help the student with
his difficulties. At The University of Michigan, recordings are
being made of the student responses that call for monitor in-
terference and also of the assistance provided, in order to study
and improve this phase of the instruction.

Hutchinson [13] has summarized the advantages of a good
language laboratory. It provides: (1) active simultaneous participation of all students; (2) a variety of native voices, un-
tiring models; (3) for individual differences, lessons adapted
to students, which they follow at their own rate; (4) teacher
freedom from tedious drilling routines; (5) teacher opportunity to correct students without interrupting others; (6)
equal hearing conditions for all students; (7) privacy, reducing inhibitions and distractions; (8) facilities for group test-

[13] Joseph C. Hutchinson, "Modern Foreign Languages in High
School: The Language Laboratory," *Review of Educational Research,
op. cit.,* Chap. 5.

ing of listening and speaking skills; (9) possibilities for co-
ordinating audio and visual materials; and (10) aid to
teachers in improving their audio-lingual proficiency. In addition it provides instruction in languages for which there may
be no teachers available, for it is an instructional device, not
merely an aid, in that it has direct responsibility for a part in
the teaching.

If the audio-lingual method alone is used, those who finish
the training have not learned to read and write the foreign
language—in this sense they are illiterates. With the traditional course organization, as has been noted, there is no
place for them to go, since the usual language classes are
made up of students who cannot speak or understand the
language and are laboring through the usual rules and para-
digms that few native users of the language know. This condition is being corrected, however, as more and more students
have the audio-lingual training. The language laboratory itself
is undergoing a transformation in process by becoming a complex teaching machine that will add the reading and writing
skills to its repertoire. Already language lessons are being programmed, and it is likely that these skills will be taught much
more effectively than they have been in the past.

As is well known, language instruction in American schools
has not been given high priority partly because few students
had any use for it, and partly because the grammatical
methods of instruction, following the Latin model, were un-
appealing and usually left the student unable either to speak
or to read the language. A few were able to translate slowly
and laboriously. Even this ability was soon lost through dis-
use, particularly since only language majors studied any one
language more than a year or two, enough to give them the
Carnegie units for college entrance—if they went to college.

The emphasis of the linguists and the language laboratories
is not on grammar—on declensions, conjugations, and rules.
The student does not learn to *talk about* the language, he

learns to *use* it. Nor is the emphasis on translation. They give primacy to the spoken language on the assumption that people should learn a second or third language in much the same way that they learn their own, first by hearing (and understanding), followed by speaking, reading, and writing, in that order. The language laboratory at present takes care of the first two stages, although the hearing and saying stages proceed more or less concurrently.

Student behavior in the language laboratory may be summarized as follows:

Get set: Readiness for the lessons being studied is assured by testing and previous progress, and often aided by preliminary warming up, perhaps including music or pictures from the country that uses the language being studied.

Listen: Language sounds (phonemes) are presented separately, in words, and in sentences.

Discriminate: Differences that make a difference in the new language are emphasized, e.g., Spanish-speaking students learning English may confuse *bet* and *bit;* Japanese students *lamb* and *ram,* English-speaking students the Spanish *r,* and so on.

Respond: Practice follows in imitating or echoing the foreign sounds, since practically all of them are different from the English sounds. Verbal instruction can reduce the trial-and-error process here as in other motor skills. Echoing includes practice in intonation, the pitch changes in spoken sentences.

Drill: Responses are repeated over and over in different contexts.

Practice patterns: Lexical meanings are introduced by inserting them in different parts or "slots" of stock sentences.

Correct through feedback: Throughout, the student compares his pronunciation with that of the recorded voice of the native speaker and, through progressive approximations, relatively quickly acquires the correct pronunciation.

Drill more: The student repeats sounds, words, passages, questions.

Reinforce: Improved and strengthened responses are established as a result of immediate correction, and the attendant satisfaction increases motivation.

Test: Each response is a test, but cleverly designed paper-and-pencil tests reveal the progress each student is actually making.

Progress: The student proceeds at his own rate. If he is absent, on his return he begins where he left off.

Habituate: Review experiences and continuing effort help the student to make his responses automatic so that he no longer has to think about them but only about what he is saying.

Naturally these are not to be regarded as successive steps but rather as elements of the process that reveals the way in which the language laboratory can follow the learning diagram presented earlier, and systematically build language competence. The meaning of the word *course* in this connection is understandably vague since the process is continuous, and any break merely signifies that in view of the other things students have to do, progress to some defined point (a certain number of pages or recordings covered, or clock hours spent) will be expected in a semester or year, though some may reach that point more quickly and others will have to put in extra time, or not cover so much ground. Language learning is basically skill behavior. A language is a pre-existing structural system to be acquired. There is no occasion for creativity, only for mistakes. The mistakes must be corrected, right responses taught, habituated, made automatic.

Some say that language skill is not properly viewed as college work, that it is mastered by children in their native country and should be acquired in the elementary and secondary schools, thus leaving instruction in the literature and culture of a country for the colleges to carry on in the language of that country, with minimal attention being given to the language itself. College students who have not attained sufficient competence for such instruction may use the language laboratory until they have, but not for "college credit." Whether or not this goal will be achieved no one can now say. It does present a challenge to the schools which now have difficulty in developing competence in their students even in their native language. It is a goal worth striving for and does not preclude the possibility of practice at any level in the expressive use of the language as literature or for acquiring knowledge in any field. But for those purposes, other methods and materials than the present language laboratory will be employed.

Language teachers of the future will need to be better prepared than they are today, but there will be greater satisfaction in leading discussions and reading literature in the foreign language with students who have already mastered the basic auditory and linguistic skills.

Perhaps relatively undue attention has been given to language instruction. But here is where the break-through has occurred. New linguistic procedures and automated techniques make it a special case. It is more than likely that similar advances in other subjects will be made. Of course, science laboratories, art rooms, shops, and gymnasiums have for some time had a place in American schools, but it is doubtful if these facilities have been fully exploited in the interest of effective learning. The mathematics workroom or laboratory is on the way. English, except as it is taught as a foreign language, has yet to profit in any systematic way from the developments in foreign language learning. Social studies as a school subject has had an uncertain career, but the ideals of continuity and proficiency coupled with the potentials of modern technology may produce desirable changes. Suggestions [14] for a high school social science workroom include "calculating machines for tabulating research data, type-

[14] J. Lloyd Trump in National Association of Secondary School Principals, op. cit., p. 388.

writers, equipment for making maps and charts, programmed learning books and machines, listening, viewing, and recording devices, books, and other materials social scientists use." The opportunity is here, details remain to be worked out.

4

Environmental Control:
The New Media

THE LANGUAGE LABORATORY, broadening into wider use as a sound laboratory (Chapter 3), is definitely a recent innovation and is quite properly classified among the new media of instruction. It has already escaped from the adjunct category, and although many improvements will no doubt be made in it, it is well beyond the experimental stage. Its use is relatively restricted, however, and its future possibilities can be fairly clearly envisioned, although its functional relationships with other media are yet to be worked out. The possibilities for using radio, television, and teaching machines, discussed in this chapter, are, on the other hand, so extensive in both the psychological and curricular dimensions that it will undoubtedly be some time before their potentialities are fully realized.

Vacuum Tube—Radio and Television

With the invention of the vacuum tube and later the transistor, the science of electronics picked up the ball and headed for goals undreamed of earlier. First came the radio in the early 'twenties, which overcame the obstacle of distance in the transmission of sound, and then television which did the same for visible events, moving the transmission from wires to airwaves. Radio developed commercially with great rapidity. According to the 1960 census, 91 per cent of American homes had radio receivers which were tuned in on an average of two hours a day. A number of cities, New York, Philadelphia, and Flint, Michigan, for example, broadcast regular educational radio programs, but its most common use in schools is in the form of a public address or an intercommunications system, the latter a constant temptation to principals which the wiser resist as often as possible.

Along with the other changes that are under way, it may be that the schools should take another look at the possibilities of radio as an instructional medium. Just as all pictures do not need motion, so all events at a distance do not require visual presentation. Surveys have shown that 80 per cent or more of a population may be reached in this way, and that in schools, radio recordings are in general more popular than live programs because of greater ease in scheduling and the opportunity to preview and to re-use them.

Why educational radio never caught on in a large way is difficult to say. To many it may not have seemed worth the effort to develop programs for radio alone. Perhaps the best answer is that the time was not ripe. This is a vague sort of assertion. It may mean more if it is stated in another way: many did not recognize the need or the possibilities. The same was true of Pressey's testing and teaching machines in the 'thirties. With the population explosion and the consequent teacher shortages, complacency gave way to concern.

The popular attacks on education, although much of the opinion expressed was uninformed, tended to increase public interest in educational problems. The need was recognized for more knowledge in view of the rapid developments in the sciences, and the general interest in world events outside the confines of the Western tradition. Technology developed rapidly in other areas, culminating in Sputnik, which dramatically called attention to the forty-year-long efforts of Russia to "overtake and surpass" the Western nations, with the consequent demand for more science, mathematics, and languages and the counter demand for more knowledge of the humanities. As a consequence of these events, a different climate developed. The earlier, unfortunate complacency disappeared. The possibilities hitherto lying dormant in the older technologies are now being examined, as are the newer, not only in the matter of mechanical apparatus but also in personnel organization. Probably no one device or process alone is of sufficient value to be inserted into the traditional school system. But all together, and integrated into the total educational system, each with its proper part to play, they should and can make definite and much-needed improvements.

TELEVISION AS A MEDIUM OF INSTRUCTION

There is probably no better illustration of the rapidity with which innovations are adopted when substantial profits are likely to accrue than in the development of commercial television. In a relatively brief time, the ten years between 1950 and 1960, 88 per cent of American homes were equipped with receiving sets, and the antennas above the rooftops have become a more familiar cultural symbol than church spires or tall chimneys.

Commercial Television

It has been estimated on the basis of numerous studies that children of public school age spend an average of two to four hours a day watching television. Little is known about the effects of excessive viewing of the products of the commercial networks with their partiality for the "pistol pictures," showing in vivid detail all manner of crime and mayhem. At least

it can be said that even if for many children they do no positive harm, they can hardly do much good, especially in view
of the world's riches that remain unexplored by the children
who spend nearly all their out-of-school hours glued to the
TV screen. Whether the banal repetition of slogans of the com-
mercials makes them more or less immune to propaganda is
not known, although it is probable that they get some weird
ideas of human physiology from the diagrams of the effects
of various drugs on the brain, sinuses, and digestive system.

On the other hand as a direct consequence of commercial
radio and television, many children are much better informed
than were their parents on world events. They have watched
human operations of all kinds from the growing of rice to
the firing of rockets; they have visited far-off countries and
seen their leaders in action. They have witnessed sporting
events, highly competent musical and dramatic productions,
and the discussion of political and social problems by those
responsible for dealing with them. As a consequence, the
teacher's presentations may seem a bit inadequate. And yet
the school curriculum has made little or no adjustment to
this rich background of vicarious experience.

But, it is all passive consumption, not active participation.
The great majority of today's children have not set traps, fed
chickens, milked cows, cooked a dinner, driven a horse, cut
corn, picked fruit, sold newspapers, or even played sandlot
baseball. Some of the activities of the modern school are set
up to provide some of the direct experience with reality that
their parents, or at least their grandparents, had in their day.

Educational Television

In addition to regular commercial programs the networks
and local stations frequently carry educational and cultural
programs as a public service. The first thoroughgoing instructional program to appear on a national network was given the
name *Continental Classroom*. In 1958, a course in *Atomic*

Age Physics was broadcast over commercial and educational stations, sponsored by the American Association of Colleges for Teacher Education. The objective was primarily to upgrade science teachers, of whom some 40,000 out of the nation's 70,000 enrolled, in spite of the early morning hour (6:00 A.M.), as did also some 4,000 students in 250 colleges and universities which gave academic credit for the course. *Modern Chemistry* was offered the following year by the newly organized Learning Resources Institute, supported financially by grants from a number of foundations and industries, and with the backing of a dozen or more national professional organizations. So great was the success of this innovation that a year later a course in *Contemporary Mathematics* (Modern Algebra, and Probability and Statistics) was offered, while added courses in *The New Biology, The American Economy*, and *Literature of the Western World* were planned for the next three years, with the active support of the respective national professional organizations. In the fall of 1961 the Learning Resources Institute transferred its program and *The New Biology* to another network, using the series title, *College of the Air*, while *Continental Classroom* continued on its old channel with a series called *American Government*, presented in color.

In addition to the regular channels more than fifty educational television channels are in use throughout the country. Since many operate on ultra-high frequency (UHF), they require specially equipped receivers. But in spite of this, the audiences run into the millions. Supported usually by industrial, philanthropic, and educational organizations, their programs include courses for children and adults as well as many of artistic and cultural interest.

In 1961 there began an educational experiment so bizarre that even Jules Verne would have rejected the idea if it had occurred to him. Lessons prepared in television studios the year before and recorded on video tape were beamed from an airplane 23,000 feet up. This is MPATI, the Midwest Program in Airborn Television Instruction. And just to make sure, a stand-by plane was kept in readiness to take off should there be any trouble with the first, for "the show must go on." The reason for this cerulean podium is simple: it was actually less expensive than providing booster stations for special UHF channels for the potential audience of 5 million pupils in 13,000 schools within a radius of some 200 miles. The center of the circle, Montpelier, Indiana, was chosen because it is not far from Purdue University, which was selected as the operation center, and because the air over Montpelier was found to be unusually free from established air-lanes. Twenty-four half-hour lessons at the elementary level, four at the secondary, and the available Continental Classroom college-level courses were scheduled for six hours a day, four days a week. The cost of 7 million dollars ($4\frac{1}{2}$ borne by the Ford Foundation and the remainder subscribed by various industries) may seem excessive. But this was a first trial, and for 5 million pupils it does not add up to so much per pupil. In 1962, MPATI received a final grant of 7.5 million dollars from the Ford Foundation to be budgeted in decreasing amounts over the next four years. Income from fees from the member schools at the rate of approximately one dollar per pupil is expected gradually to take over support of the operation. Plans were laid for the purchase of two new planes that will fly 5,000 feet higher and so increase the reception area by one-third. Also, two and perhaps four new channels will be added thus enlarging the potential patronage still further.

Two hundred educators collaborated in one way or another in the project, the most expert lecture-demonstration teachers that could be found were selected to present the lessons, given free time to prepare for them, and an allowance for demonstration materials and other instructional aids. As a consequence, many children can now have instruction that would not otherwise be available to them, and many teachers are able to observe better teaching than they are accustomed to provide. In a survey of 987 teachers using MPATI in their classrooms, 94 per cent rated TV teaching methods as good or excellent, 96 per cent rated the lesson material as important or very important, and 97 per cent rated the use of visuals in the telecasts as effective or very effective. Other studies showed that TV instruction compared favorably with regular classroom instruction.

Few are willing to predict the future of educational television. Some oppose the idea of standardized content on general principles. Others report that the lessons do not fit the grades for which they are intended: in some schools they are too difficult, in others the material has already been covered. Still others wonder why the school budget should bear the brunt of double instruction, paying for both television and a regular teacher. Answers to the last question sound almost like double talk: on the one hand, TV lessons supply small schools with courses for which there is no qualified teacher, and on the other, the teacher watching the screen with the class is not only upgraded but he is needed to discuss the TV content with the class after the showing. Since the traditional classroom system does not allow teachers to observe each other teach, the opportunity to observe good teaching via TV is undoubtedly a valuable experience, particularly for students in training or beginning teachers. Apart from the training function, it is still uncertain whether either the teacher or ETV should be self-sufficient, or whether both are needed. There are other alternatives depending on the possibilities of a general reorganization of educational processes.

Closed-Circuit Television

In addition to the national networks and local stations and the educational television stations (ETV), there are three or four hundred closed-circuit installations (CCTV) operated chiefly by various educational institutions, and ranging in size from state-wide coverage to those that hook up a room or two with a TV camera. If it is not desired to give live programs, the camera is not necessary, only a projector for showing video tape recordings, with cables connecting the classrooms. The on-the-spot TV camera gives students in classroom or auditorium close-up views of lecture demonstrations, e.g., of biological dissections and microscope slides, and opportunities to observe activities in near-by rooms or buildings. Large units are used for teaching full-length courses, thus far usually on an experimental basis. An extension of this plan uses microwave instead of cable connections, permitting state-wide hook-up of a number of institutions so that a course can be given on one campus and beamed to several others.

The Role of ETV

Like other audio-visual instruction, television is most effective in the perceptual phases of learning, in providing sensory experiences, pointing up significant cues, and more broadly, orienting the student, informing him, and perhaps inspiring him to carry his learning further. There is still some question as to whether pictures should be used to explain words, or words should be used to explain pictures, and the matter is not yet resolved. However, ETV usually features the lecture in spite of the criticisms of this form of instruction. While there is greater flexibility in the use of CCTV, with large-scale presentation there is no feedback to the lecturer or demonstrator to tell him how he is doing. He can give no examinations on what he has covered (though questions may be telecast for local teachers to score). There is no opportunity for discussion and the expression of student opinion until after the show is over, and no way to vary the flow of discourse for the benefit of student differences. In general, then, ETV is less effective when the feedback response is important, and when discussion and give-and-take between the student and the instructor are needed.

While the educational motion picture usually features the objects or events being shown, perhaps with an unseen narrator or commentator, educational television usually features the lecturer. For the sake of continuity and the personal influence that a teacher on a screen can provide, it is probably best to retain him, but it may well be that future productions will upstage him somewhat. He can still point to his graphs and charts and manipulate his apparatus, but he should probably more often allow the events he is describing to take over if the potentialities of the medium are to be fully exploited. There are endless possibilities not only for the dramatic portrayal of scenes from nature and of human action, but for a variety of shots—industrial plants and processes, government agencies in action, and close-ups of all manner of processes in various vocational, social, and cultural activities. In addition, the pedagogical possibilities of animated speaking cartoon figures, dialogue, guest speakers, panel discussions, and explanations to a dead-pan accomplice who makes anticipated mistakes can be further exploited, in addition to the usual maps, charts and diagrams, original documents, photographs, sketches, scientific equipment, and artifacts from museums, libraries, and historical societies. Ingenuity in the use of the varied resources adds the "you are there" flavor of reality. Manuals, syllabuses, and reference readings for teachers and students give permanence to what is presented, and as has long been done, the presentation can be followed by discussion, debate, and student projects, or by teaching machines or other programmed instruction, if so desired, to reinforce the learning.

The potential value of the medium is in a way symbolized by the fact that two international conferences were held in 1961, the first under the auspices of UNESCO and the U. S. Office of Education at which representatives of educational radio and television organizations from more than forty nations met to promote international cooperation and exchange in the development of television in their several countries. To summarize, the chief advantage of educational television is that it can carry instruction to different classrooms where it might not otherwise be provided, or where it would have to be repeated. It can provide superior lecture demonstrations for extensive curricular content, and it makes possible close-up views of what is being demonstrated and of on-going events for class observation. Beyond this, it has the advantage of all audio-visual instruction, that of enhancing the value of perceptual instruction.

There are naturally some disadvantages. The chief one is that it is a viewing and listening device only. While it is going on, no further action is possible. If a student is uninterested, he may prefer his own daydreams, or he may use the TV period to catch up on his sleep, but this is not unheard of even with a "live" lecturer. The small size of the screen requires several spaced at intervals around the room; although the image may be magnified, for showing on a large screen, the definition is not so clear. There can be no audience participation, no opportunity as with a book to pause and reflect on what has been said, and notes are likely to be scanty because one must watch the picture, while it is not necessary to watch a lecturer. Perhaps the chief disadvantage is that the instructor proceeds at his own rate, and there is no possibility of adapting instruction to individual differences among the viewers in intelligence or background. For this reason viewers should not necessarily be a grade or class, but a group of students who are ready for the instruction that is to be so provided. It is quite possible to transfer video tape to 8-mm sound film with cartridge loading to be used by small groups or even by individuals when they are ready.

Thus far the claims of success for television instruction are moderate both on the basis of economy and of student achievement. It has not reduced instructional costs but this was hardly to be expected in view of the expense of initial installations which, however, can be used for some time to come; and many lessons can be repeated from kinescope recordings. It may be that with newer types of class organization, team teaching, and parallel use of other media, and the kinescope revisions, the costs will not be materially reduced. It seems likely, however, that the future increase in school population will not increase costs as much as would be the case without television. If the quality of instruction is at the same time improved, as at present seems likely, its place in education is assured.

While student achievement has not markedly increased, TV instruction is at least as effective as conventional classroom techniques.[1] The reasons for the slight differences found are not far to seek. One is that students can usually read in textbooks what they are supposed to learn to make up for any differences in what has been presented to them. A second reason is that the perceptual contribution of television is not tested by the instruments used, usually the regular course examination. A third reason for only moderate gains, in some cases at least, is that the equipment has been inadequate or not properly installed or kept up. In order to save a little money, the number of cameras or their quality has sometimes not been what it should be, the technicians have not had the needed skill, too little time or care has been given to the preparation of the script, or the best advantage has not been taken of the possibilities of the medium. A fourth reason for only moderate success may be that the talent chosen for appearance before the cameras has in some cases been less than adequate. One such lecturer was described as "just another teacher with a blackboard." The consensus of opinion seems to favor using a competent teacher trained for television rather than a television actor with a prepared script, but many take the op-

[1] William H. Allen, *Television for California Schools,* Bulletin of the California State Department of Education, Vol. 39, No. 4 (April, 1960).

posite position. While scholarship is no guarantee of teaching ability, as every collegian knows, even the best teachers selected for television appearance require training. They must have or acquire some of the actor's skills, a well modulated voice, clear enunciation, avoidance of mannerisms and other meaningless movements, expressive features, and the like. Television may magnify the defects of the teacher instead of increasing his effectiveness.

Meanwhile, schools within range of televised lessons can advantageously arrange to use them, giving everyone practice and experience with the medium. And school systems can well experiment with a television camera wired to connect with a few rooms. Or there may at first be no need of a camera for live programs, only kinescope projection with cable connections to rooms with receiving sets. The planning that will be necessary may be a good way to initiate cooperation for other technological improvements. And universities can train teachers in the use of the medium, develop ideas for more effective television instruction, and conduct experiments that may result in techniques to increase its effectiveness in promoting learning of different subjects and parts of subjects by students of different ages, abilities, and interests. Specifications for new school buildings should include conduits for television cables since during construction the additional cost is minimal. Even if there is no immediate expectation of employing television, continuing developments will be likely to win local converts and later make its use mandatory.

Many do not realize the present possibilities of the medium. Lewis [2] lists the following, some of which have been discussed, but all are included here by way of summary:

1. Centralized electronic distribution of motion picture films and other visuals direct to where it is wanted

[2] For a detailed description of technical considerations, see Philip Lewis, *Education Television Guide Book* (New York, McGraw-Hill Book Co., Inc., 1961).

2. Remote monitoring of corridors, play, and other areas

3. Central storage of personnel records or other data that are immediately available for remote visual examination or direct copying from the TV screen

4. Electronic hook-up of widely separated school buildings or locations for conference purposes

5. Ease of pupil viewing or demonstration procedures in shops and laboratories

6. Extension and expansion of audience and spectator facilities

7. Kinescope or video-tape recordings of presentations and programs for repeated use later the same day or in the future

In the experimental stage are two-way television, systems of remote and almost instantaneous measurement of student reaction, and portable, inexpensive video-tape recording apparatus.

PROGRAMMED LEARNING AND TEACHING MACHINES

The teaching machine [3] is the only one of the mechanical inventions noted in Chapter III that was originally designed solely for educational purposes. It provides the necessary supplement to television and other audio-visual materials in that it makes the student an active participant in learning instead of a passive recipient. It requires him to respond successively to many questions, and it furnishes feedback on the correctness of his responses.

Many kinds of machines have been invented [4] and are on

[3] Neither teaching machine nor learning machine is a satisfactory name for this invention because it neither teaches nor learns. Since the programs fed into it individualize instruction, it has been called a tutoring machine, and more exactly and awkwardly, a self- (or auto-) instructional device. For the present, however, it looks as if it will be a teaching machine.

[4] See Sam and Beryl Epstein, *The First Book of Teaching Machines* (New York, Franklin Watts, Inc., 1961). This little book contains a number of excellent illustrations.

the market, some sixty or so companies already have them to sell, ranging from simple devices in which the program sheets are inserted and moved up by hand, including more complex inventions that have levers or knobs to move the program sheets or microfilm, and that show the answers and also record mistakes, to highly complex electronic devices with taped comments on them that admonish the student in an avuncular fashion. Several hundred thousand have already been sold and the trade anticipates a 50 million dollar business in ten years. Others are not so enthusiastic, like the mother who exclaimed, "A machine to teach my child? Not on your life! A child needs human warmth." By the same token she would not want her child to learn from books. Some have asked somewhat fearfully whether the machine will replace the teacher. Stated in this way, this is a foolish question although some intelligent men have attempted to answer it. Some say yes, that teachers who fear they will be replaced probably should be. They go on to describe the possibilities of electronically operated computers. Some, perhaps to reassure the profession, say no, that it will only relieve the teacher of the onerous task of drilling pupils and leave him more time for real teaching. Neither of these answers is an honest one because the meaning of the question is not clear. What is meant by "the teacher"? For almost everyone it suggests the stereotype previously mentioned. *The* teacher-*the* classroom stereotype, it can confidently be predicted, will be less frequent in actuality than it is at present.

And what is meant by "replace"? Rewording the question clarifies it. Will machines do many of the things teachers now do? The answer here is an unqualified affirmative, even with the addition—and do them better. The typewriter and printing press, the adding machine and computer are faster and more accurate than human scribes and accountants. But does this mean that machines will replace school personnel? Obviously not. There will no doubt be fewer "general practitioners," and more people who are specialists whether or not they are called teachers. We already have curriculum specialists, audio-visualists, school librarians, visiting teachers, counselors, and school psychologists, to say nothing of the subject matter specialists. Others may be expected to develop.

And so far as the machines are concerned, they are not so important as the programs they carry. Actually, programs do not have to be presented by machines at all. They can be printed in books, so-called programmed texts. The question as to which is the more satisfactory way to present a program, by machine [5] or textbook, has not been satisfactorily answered. Machines are probably more attractive to children, perhaps because of their so-called toy appeal. They are convenient to use because frequent page turning is eliminated. Furthermore, on most machines it is not so easy for the student to read the answers provided before writing them down, and the overt manipulation of the shift mechanism theoretically is an aid to reinforcement, although this is not borne out by experiments. The use of microfilm gives promise of reducing the sheer bulk of paper now used in machines and programmed textbooks alike, and it is likewise favored for recording student errors and for connection with other devices including tape and film.

On the other hand, machines are expensive and mechanical difficulties arise, thus adding maintenance costs. Program sheets do not fit equally well into different types of machines and the paper may tear. Mature students may prefer the book form, since this is what they are used to, or, when the novelty has worn off, may not care to fool around with a machine. For short supplementary programs, the textbook format is likely to be all that is needed.

[5] See Lumsdaine and Glaser, *op. cit.*, especially papers by B. F. Skinner, Douglas Porter, James G. Holland, Skinner and Holland, Simon Ramo, and James D. Finn.

Although much attention has been given to the design of different kinds of machines, whatever the method of presentation, it is important that the program be good. For it serves a dual function, that of a tutor who asks questions in a kind of Socratic fashion [6] to lead the student step-by-step to further knowledge and understanding, and also that of the workbook which perhaps quizzes the student more systematically and calls for written answers. But it does these things more effectively than classroom teacher and workbook. "The teacher" cannot possibly give individual attention to the oral and written answers of all the pupils in a class, nor are his questions or those in the workbook likely to be so carefully prepared and sequentially arranged as are the self-instructional programs.

Characteristics of Self-Instructional Devices

The chief characteristics of good programmed instruction of the so-called linear type (the branching type will be described later), may be placed in six categories:

1. *Small sequential steps.* Each item of the program is so stated that on the basis of what has preceded, nearly all the students can respond to approximately 90 per cent of them correctly. And yet after they have proceeded a short distance, they are answering questions they could not have answered previously. If many students fail an item, it is not the student but the item that is at fault; it may be ambiguous or irrelevant, or it may require additional items to lead up to it. A carefully prepared program usually needs three or four trial runs, the first perhaps on a single student, and consequent revisions before it is ready for use.

2. *Learner response.* The learner may respond by pushing a button to indicate his *recognition* of the correct answers to multiple-choice items, the scheme used by S. L. Pressey with his pioneer teaching machines in the early 'thirties and char-

[6] *Cf.* pp. 105, 106.

acteristic of some of the devices today. Or he may *write in* a word or a few words, the "constructed response," to indicate his *recall*. This is the plan of the familiar completion test preferred by B. F. Skinner, for which his machines were designed. In either case, the learner responds, he does something, and so he learns and gives evidence that he is learning.

3. *Self-pacing*. The learner can proceed at his own rate. If he needs to stop and think for a while, he may do so without fear of disparaging remarks from his classmates or from the teacher. Thus undesirable mediating conditions are minimized. If he is a fast learner, he can forge ahead, a satisfying experience for him because there is no one to think he is showing off, and his success does not penalize others with lower marks. Some have made the mistake of assigning a certain fraction of a program to be covered per class period. This procedure, of course, negates its self-pacing value. It is probable that very slow students and perhaps the very bright could profit by special programs, the first simpler and more repetitious, the second with larger steps; but there is yet no experimentation to decide this matter.

4. *Feedback*. Knowledge of results, that is, of the response and its consequences, is essential in learning. With programmed instruction the learner is informed at once whether or not his response is correct, while in the usual school situation, only the student who is reciting may get this information, and he may not. If written work is corrected and returned, he learns of his errors a day or several days later, and by then he is likely to have lost interest.

5. *Reinforcement*. Closely related to knowledge of results is the reinforcement of the student's response, which in some obscure way is found to strengthen learning. Thorndike spoke of the confirming reaction of the learner. Pavlov reinforced the salivary responses of the dogs he conditioned with food, as did Skinner the rats and pigeons. The latter referred to the

"emitted" response as whatever the subject does whether or not we know what the stimulus was that produced it. If the emitted response was the "correct" one, i.e., the one desired by the experimenter, it was immediately reinforced, as was any response that was more nearly correct than a preceding one. The name *trial-and-error learning* implies that the learner was trying to do something, which might or might not be the case. The term *successive approximations* is more accurate since it implies the reinforcing of successive units of behavior. As has been noted, the coach's encouragement does the same thing when he says, "That's the idea . . . that's better . . . try again."

The teacher in the classroom is handicapped by the number of pupils and the number of their responses. He cannot possibly reinforce each response. But the machine can. Immediately after making his response, the student is able to confirm it by comparing it with the correct answer. Some opine that the confirmation is strengthened by the action of pulling a lever or turning a knob to expose the next item in the program. While what is called reinforcement is some external event, the process is actually an internal response of the learner. Even when there is no machine and no one around, there is an inner realization on the part of the student that he is responding correctly and getting along all right.

6. *Product evaluation.* The teaching machine also usually provides a record of the student's errors and hence of his performance. It would seem inadvisable to use this record as a basis for marking, since this would tend to exert pressure on the slow pupil so that he might become as frustrated as in the ordinary classroom. A rerun or review items will give him an opportunity to correct the errors, but he may be improperly classified and given too difficult a program. The fast student should finish with few mistakes and in much less time than the year usually apportioned to a course. If he is

progressing satisfactorily in other subjects, he should go ahead and not be bound by what is considered a "year's work" for average students.

Response Modes:[7] Multiple-Choice vs. Constructed Response

Some teaching machines, following the Skinnerian plan, provide a place for the student to write in his constructed response, which is then rolled up under a small window where he cannot change it, but where it can be compared with the right answer that comes into view. Others, like Pressey's original device, have keys for the student to press to indicate his choice from a series of answers.

Both types of questions can be presented also in book form, for which the student can record his answers on a separate answer sheet. These can be checked by a teacher or by a chemical or mechanical device like Pressey's early inventions.[8] He is thus informed when a response is incorrect, so he keeps on marking until he gets the right answer. When the programmed textbook [9] is used, the first frame appears, say, at the top of the first right-hand page, page 1, the second (with the correct answer for the *first* frame), at the top of page 3. At the end of the chapter or booklet, the student returns to page 1 for the next frame, which appears directly under the first, and so on. There are usually four or five frames per page. When

[7] Harry F. Silberman in the *Review of Educational Research, op. cit.,* pp. 180–183.

[8] S. L. Pressey, "Development and Appraisal of Devices Providing Immediate Automatic Scoring of Objective Tests and Concomitant Self-Instructions," in Wendell I. Smith and J. William Moore, eds., *Programmed Learning* (New York, D. Van Nostrand Co., Inc., 1962), pp. 111–149; or in Lumsdaine and Glaser, *op. cit.,* pp. 69–88 (see also pp. 32–58).

[9] L. E. Homme and R. Glaser, "Relationship between the Programmed Textbook and Teaching Machines," paper presented at the Conference on Automated Teaching of Verbal and Symbolic Skills, University of Pennsylvania, 1958.

the right-hand pages are completed, the student goes back to the beginning and follows the left-hand pages in the same way, always writing down his answers, perhaps in a separate note-book or on a roll of paper, before turning to the next page to check the accuracy of his answers.

There are variations of this format. The student may follow consecutive instead of alternate pages. Sometimes the book is divided into sections so that after, say, twenty pages, he will return to page 1 and proceed to page 20 on the second row of frames, and so on, so that when all the frames on pages 1-20 are completed, he will continue on page 21. Some pro-grammed books present the frames in vertical columns, four or five to a large page, a scheme which makes frequent page-turning unnecessary. But this requires the use of a shield of some kind which the student is supposed to slide down the column to cover the answers that are below each item. This scheme should probably be used only for mature students who recognize the value of writing their responses first, or if they do look ahead, make it a point to learn the right answers as they go along, perhaps with inner rehearsal. This is prob-ably what occurred in the experiments in which subjects who did not write down the answers came out about as well as those who did. Short programs (or programs in process of construction) can well be typed on 3 by 5 cards with the answer on the reverse side. In using these the student writes his answers on a separate sheet before turning the card over for checking and reinforcement.

Those who favor the multiple-choice procedure argue that it is convenient, easy to score, more easily permits branching, that the student learns from his mistakes, and that it is im-portant to force him to make fine discriminations among known choices. Those opposed argue that the student is as likely to learn his mistakes as the right choices, that the alternative choices are apt to be artificially constructed distractions, and that when confronted with a row of keys, some students are likely to press them at random to see what happens, sometimes without even reading the question.

The basic difference between the two forms, of course, is that the constructed response requires that the learner think up or *recall* the answer, while the multiple-choice response requires only that he *recognize* it among the wrong answers. (An exception is found in cases in which the student must compute the answer.) A decision as to which form to use would, therefore, seem to depend on the kind of behavior expected of the learner, recall or recognition. If he is too young to write, or if the important thing for him to do is to mark which of the given answers is the same as the one he has just computed, to learn to discriminate similar objects or terms that he might otherwise confuse, or decide between known alternatives (a common enough life situation), then the multiple-choice procedure would be indicated. If, on the other hand, the objective of the instruction requires that the learner *know,* that he make the correct associations himself, then this is what he should learn to do, and the constructed response is called for. It should be emphasized, however, that the purpose is not to test the student, but to teach him.

It may not always be easy to decide which kind of behavior is more important, especially for a whole unit of instruction. This should not be necessary, however, because any one program might well include both forms. The student could just as well "write in" his choice of two or more given alternatives as he could a response he has thought up or recalled. So, although a push-button machine would necessarily require multiple-choice questions, a write-in machine or programmed textbook could be used for either form.

Linear Programs vs. Branching

Whether prepared for constructed-response or multiple-choice questions, for machine or book format, the linear program is presented in small sequential steps, and the student gives his answer, which is reinforced if it is correct. The procedure has been challenged by N. A. Crowder [10] and his followers, who advocate the so-called branching program. In it, the program frames are of varying length and usually contain considerably more exposition than the Skinnerian, perhaps a whole page. On this account, and also because the students answer questions in different sequences, they present problems to those designing machines, calling as they do for electronic devices. The books in which they are usually presented are somewhat like the programmed texts but with a difference, which has resulted in their being called scrambled books. They have the trade name of Tutor Texts. The branching technique contains multiple-choice items based on the expository material which the student first reads. He then indicates his choice, beside which is the number of a page farther on to which he refers. He may there find that his answer was correct, in which case he goes on to the next item. If he finds his answer was incorrect, a number refers him to a different page where he is told what his error was and what he should do about it. He is then referred back to the page of the original item which he tries again. If he is wrong again, he is referred to still a different page that puts him straight on that one, and so on. This is the process by which he supposedly learns from his mistakes.

Crowder refers to this kind of branching as intrinsic because whatever answer a student chooses, his next move is determined by the programmed material. What he next does depends on his immediately preceding choice. When other data are brought in to help determine what the student should do next, such as his intelligence or series of earlier responses, the branching is called extrinsic. This is comparable to what a

[10] See Norman A. Crowder, "Intrinsically Programmed Materials for Teaching Complex Skills and Concepts," paper read at the American Psychological Association, Washington, D.C. (August, 1958); also, N. A. Crowder, "Intrinsic and Extrinsic Programming," in Coulson, *op. cit.*, pp. 58–66.

tutor might do when he says, "Let's leave that for a while; you'll be ready for it when you have done this next assignment." But for programming, a rather complicated machine is needed, like the AutoTutor Mark II or a computer. Both intrinsic and extrinsic branching techniques he terms responsive, that is, responsive to the student's behavior. The Skinnerian linear type of program he terms nonresponsive.

Crowder [11] states that "a routine question" on a routine step in the program should serve:

1. to determine whether the student has learned the material just presented;
2. to select appropriate corrective material if the student has not learned;
3. to provide desirable practice with the concept involved;
4. to keep the student actively working at the material; and
5. to fill a desirable motivational purpose if the student answers the question correctly.

It is evident that the construction of such programs is no simple task, even if, as Crowder says, while "for a routine program no more of the 15 per cent of the students should select a wrong answer, a major program branch might have a question that would be failed by 90 per cent of the students."

The Skinnerians hold that it is better to teach him correctly in the first place instead of confusing him by showing him so many wrong answers. On the other hand it is argued that much of man's ignorance consists not in the absence of knowledge but in his acceptance of statements that are not so.

Among the advantages urged for the branching technique are the following:

1. As compared with the linear, multiple-choice procedure, the learner is not merely blocked by his wrong answers and forced to guess again. He is told why he is wrong, misunderstandings are cleared up, and needed information supplied.

[11] N. A. Crowder in Coulson, *op. cit.*, pp. 58–66.

2. The student who knows the answers can move along rapidly in linear fashion, by not taking time to explore the branches. The steps, too, are longer than they are in the linear, constructed-response form, which all students must take one by one. Even if a speeding student merely guesses the right answer, this answer is reinforced and sometimes elaborated somewhat by the comment on the page to which his response leads.

3. The student has some choice as to how deeply he wishes to go into the matter being explained.

4. The branching type is especially effective when fine discriminations between known alternatives are required, and when cues are likely to be confused and are clarified by the explanations given.

5. While linear methods may be quite satisfactory for teaching facts and concepts, branching methods are better for dealing with opinions and implications.[12]

It could be argued, however, that the greater portion of school learning is of the facts and concepts kind, including language learning, and that on this basis the consideration of opinions and implications might better be left to group discussions. Of course, a program for any topic or course could contain a combination of the two procedures, using the one that is more satisfactory for any part of the content. Either technique can be elaborated by supplementing the usual frame with what is called a panel—a separate information sheet which might at times become a picture, map, film, book, or other source material.

In any case, the instrument should not dictate the method, but rather the method should be selected that influences the learner in a particular situation to do what produces the desired learning. It is quite probable that for some kinds of content

[12] For samples of both kinds of programs, see David Cram, *Explaining Teaching Machines and Programming* (San Francisco, Fearon Publishers, Inc., 1961).

there is an advantage in knowing that certain statements are false, and why. There is no final answer as to the superiority of the linear *versus* the branching program, and decisive experiments will be difficult, for any superiority of one type may also be interpreted as indicating a superior program.

Advantages of Programmed Learning

A number of advantages have been claimed for programmed learning, and for teaching machines in particular, over the usual instructional methods:

1. Learning is more rapid. Unlike the results obtained from television, almost all studies report increased speed in coverage and higher scores on regular tests given both immediately and after a time lapse. This may be partly due to the reduction or elimination of distractions.

2. Learning is enjoyable. For the relatively short periods of time machines have been used, student attitudes have been generally favorable. The machines interact with the students, they have a kind of toy appeal, they are not impatient, they do not tire or scold, and they provide for many pupils what is a new experience for them, the experience of success. There is satisfaction in continuous progress and in building up strength in working from simpler to more difficult tasks. Some pupils, on the other hand, do not enjoy keeping their noses to the grindstone in this way but prefer the usual classroom atmosphere in which less is expected of them.

3. Learning is adapted to individual differences. The simple steps and student pacing reduce individual differences in accomplishment so that as a consequence, with proper placement and competent programming, students of all abilities can learn. With limited tasks, over varying periods of time, they can all be brought to the same level of competence. But with open-ended tasks, the more capable students can move ahead, and in any case they are not held back to the rate of

progress of the average. The progress any one student makes may differ in different subject matter areas. It has been objected that a program aimed at the middle group is too easy for some and too hard for others, and this may be true, but perhaps not so important a consideration as some may think. The well-known inclination of the brighter and more verbally facile students toward a plausible superficiality is counteracted by their being forced to proceed step by step, but the fact that the steps are not all easy still presents a challenge, and the rapid pace at which they can travel is rewarding. Many slower students, on the other hand, can answer the questions if given time and are not under pressure or subject to embarrassment. In spite of all this, however, it is probable that the extremes of both groups will profit by programs especially designed for their level of competence.

4. Learning is directed toward specific objectives. Programs are not designed merely to "cover the course." If the objective is to provide drill on certain arithmetic processes, or linguistic formalities, the students and the machines can take over, making it unnecessary for teachers to spend their time explaining and drilling on the hundreds of details. When the objective is to compute, or to use correct forms of language, one's own or another's originality is out. Solving problems and creativity in artistic expression constitute different objectives which may be helped by appropriate programs or may call for different instructional methods.

5. Learning is retained better. If the program is well made, barring unusual circumstances, it is more nearly possible than ever before to guarantee that pupils will learn what is reasonably expected of them. Not only the form of the original presentation but also the reviews and cumulative repetitions of earlier content in different contexts make such a guarantee reasonable. They will learn it at different rates, but they will learn it. This presents the schools with an almost frightening responsibility. No longer will the teacher be the one who

"covers the course" and be satisfied when the majority of the class show by examination, as soon as it is over, that they are ignorant of large amounts of its content, presumably on the principle that what they don't know won't hurt them. It is important that program makers be assured that what is taught by their programs is worth learning. Although programmed learning is retained better, people do forget, and at varying rates. It is possible that tests on programmed material are really but measures of rate of forgetting. It would be difficult to devise a test in which the errors made it possible to distinguish between what students never knew and what they have forgotten. Perhaps the distinction is not important, but it would be an interesting subject for investigation.

A complete teaching machine system includes the following necessary components.[13]

1. Program, whether linear or branching type, prepared with due care for content, objectives, and for the machine structure, constructed not necessarily by "the teacher," but by a qualified person (or persons), and revised on the basis of one or more trials.
2. Storage, the information and questions of the program. (Sometimes referred to as library; stockpile might be a less confusing and more fitting term.) The sheer paper bulk of this material whether in the form of programmed textbooks, discs, or rolled or foldover sheets suggests that (except for electronic storage) microfilm will prove to be more convenient.
3. Display or presentation to the learner, whether by programmed book, mechanical or electronic apparatus, recordings, or simulator, or combinations of these.
4. Response by the learner of some objective or observable sort. In this respect, a teaching machine system differs radically from that of the motion picture or television. The

[13] Lawrence M. Stolurow, *Teaching by Machine*, U. S. Office of Education, Cooperative Research Monograph No. 6, 1961, p. 6.

response sought, whether recognition, recall, or performance, depends on the objectives of instruction.

5. Pacing, preferably by the learner but sometimes properly regulated by the machine on the basis of the learner's competence or the timing demands of the product.

6. Comparator, the arrangement by which the response is compared with the correct one, given either by the program or automatically.

7. Feedback, or knowledge of results or reinforcement, the means by which the appropriateness of the response is communicated to the learner either as information or reward.

8. Collator-recorder, the collection and recording of learner responses, whether right or wrong, number and type of errors, etc., with a view either to improving the program or the learner's responses. This is done by school personnel, mechanically, or electronically.

9. Selector, used with multiple response, particularly with branching programs, in the form of directions to the learner as to what part of the program to turn to following his choice of responses.

10. Computer, with almost unlimited potential for satisfying all the above requirements except preparing the programs.

It will be noted that TV satisfies the presentation requirement with standardized machine pacing and storage. The Skinner-type teaching machine adds the important learner response, feedback, and learner (and perhaps teacher) comparator. The Crowder-type branching program adds the selector function with additional storage of data for multiple choices which interpret student responses.

No one knows how many of these requirements for maximum adaptation to individual learner differences are optimum for different kinds of learning. The tutor is usually taken as the model, but there is no reason to assume that this product of the prescientific age should be held sacrosanct. It has been pointed out that in the Platonic dialogue with Meno in which Socrates proved to his satisfaction that there is no teaching but only recollection by interrogating a slave boy on the square of the hypotenuse. The boy's responses were cued from the master's questions and consisted mostly of the replies, "Yes," "Certainly," "True," "No." No test was given him later to discover whether he could go through the demonstration himself, retain it over any period of time, or creatively devise an equivalent demonstration. No detailed reports have been made of the various kinds of activities that go on with different tutors during the hour, or how effective they really are. It might be that for some kinds of learning they are actually as inefficient for the individual student as they necessarily are for large numbers.

Considerable time and money are being spent on electronic computers which provide for various kinds of feedback and branching based on the student's immediate and earlier replies and on other data. Except for experimental purposes and for developing instructional programs, computer-based instruction is as yet too expensive for common use. One estimate is a dollar an hour per student. Since a number of smaller computers are more expensive than a few big ones, there is some prospect of reducing the costs by wholesale sharing. Different models use push buttons and electronic typewriters which make it possible to hold a question until the owner gets it right, to erase, to go back, or skip one or more frames, to give the correct answer at the learner's request, to select appropriate slides, to connect with individual TV viewing screens, to branch off to easier or harder sequences, and to provide a cumulative score.

Despite these amazing imitations of the tutor's function, it is likely that for the next few years, at any rate, the educational functions of the computer will be limited chiefly to research-connected activities—processing school data, recording, retrieval, and administrative studies. Perhaps this is just as well, for much needs to be found out about the use of such procedures as response modes, step size, sequencing, branching, pacing, repetition, prompting, and confirmation.

The relative place of prompting and confirmation is one of the basic theoretical problems. Prompting is virtually a case of classical conditioning with the objective to produce the right response at the first trial by contiguous presentation with the prompt followed by its gradual withdrawal (fading or vanishing). Confirmation is a process of associating reinforcement with emitted responses resulting in progressive approximation to the correct one.

Assessment procedures,[14] too, need to be improved by attacking such problems as these instead of merely making comparisons of the use of the new media with conventional methods of instruction, often with no adequate descriptions of either, over too short a period of time, and with no adequate pretest or post-test criteria. Such studies are impossible to replicate, the differences are clouded in a host of uncontrolled variables, and owing to the restricted conditions under which they are made, it is impossible to generalize from them to other situations.

Program Format

By way of summary, the possible variations in programmed instruction can be emphasized. Different content and instructional objectives point to the desirability of choice among several forms, even in the same course of instruction. Several forms are briefly described with a simple example of each.

1. Linear, recall (Skinner, extrinsic), usually following the sentence-completion pattern. The frame is the stimulus which produces the learner's response; presentation of the correct response confirms or reinforces the learner's behavior.

[14] For detailed suggestions, see Robert Glaser and David J. Klaus, "Proficiency Measurement: Assessing Human Performance," in Gagné, *op. cit.,* pp. 418–474.

Example: A line connecting the opposite angles of a square is a diagonal. The diagonal connects the _____ angles of a square. (opposite)

2. Branching, recognition (Crowder, intrinsic), usually following the multiple-choice pattern. The extended frame informs, the required choice of answers tests; the comments on the different answers to which the student is referred explain and confirm.

Example: (After an expository paragraph), The diagonal divides a square into (1) four right angles (2) three right triangles (3) two right triangles. [(1) You answered four right angles. You are behind. These are what the square has anyway. Try again. (2) With two diagonals there are certainly at least three right triangles, but the square is not so divided. Go back and see if you can't do better. (3) Two right triangles. Right! Go ahead.]

3. Language pronunciation, repetition and comparison.

Example: "Is this man Mr. Jones?" Student repeats.

4. Language pronunciation, question and answer.

Example: "Is this man Mr. Jones?" Student answers: "This man is Mr. Jones."

5. Demonstration, imitation of manipulative skill. Successive slides picture the steps in the process either with written directions or synchronized recorded voice.

Example: "Hold the instrument in the left hand in the position shown, and insert the wire through the aperture at E. Next . . ."

6. Audio or visual presentation. Sounds, music, pictures, maps, diagrams, etc., are presented and the learner identifies or discriminates as directed.

Example: The diagonals of the square are *DB* and _____. *Or,* Which is the right angle, *BDA, DAB, ABD?*

7. Verbal presentation. Problems, paragraphs, articles, books are presented or previously read, and frames contain questions on them.

Example: The area of a square, one side of which is three feet long is (6/9/27) square feet.

8. Experience report. A visit to a museum, gallery, industry, or attendance at a play or concert; frames contain questions on the experience.

Example: At the bakery they made bread, but they also made _____ and _____.

In this as in other forms the programmer should ask questions in line with instructional objectives and not yield to the examiner's temptation to ask those it is easy to "frame."

The Place of Programmed Instruction

The question is often raised, What can be taught by self-instructional devices and what cannot? Some enthusiasts are tempted to opine that everything can be, given the proper programming. It has been noted that television seems most effective in the perceptual area of learning for purposes of general orientation and demonstration. Dale [15] has suggested that education involves "imitative reaction" and "creative inter-action," and that the former is therefore "dependent learning" and suitable for programming, while "independent" self-pro-grammed learning is not. The teaching machine is probably most effective in symbolic learning, the acquisition and use of appropriate verbal responses to verbal or pictorial stimuli, including the correct use of words and numbers, the develop-ment of concepts, and discrimination in abstract meanings. All this covers a very large part of the work of the school.

Appreciation, problem solving, motor skills and team sports, discussion skills, group planning, and social adjustment prob-

[15] Edgar Dale, "No Room for Amateurs," *Audio-Visual Instruction* 6 (May, 1961), 190–192.

ably call for additional media of instruction. The beginning stages of any subject or discipline, or a new or different part of any such subject, can probably be handled effectively by programmed materials.

A word of caution should be inserted at this point. The evaluation of instructional media is not a simple matter. People are prone to follow their prejudices and decide that one or another medium is of little value when it may have been badly misused. And the usual course examination may be an inadequate criterion. Success depends on the quality of the program, the extent to which it is adapted to the course content and the characteristics of the learner, the nature and extent of the learning task and the objectives sought, e.g., knowledge, accuracy, and speed of performance, or utilization or transfer to other situations.

The student can later strike out for himself, using whatever printed or other material may be available. The pattern of program employed should, as previously noted, be the one best suited to the specific objectives of any given instruction. Already a number of innovations are being tried. One is the information panel, a card or page the student reads, studies, or refers to before or while answering certain questions in the program. Such panels may contain lists of technical terms, expository or descriptive matter, charts, diagrams, drawings, pictures or maps, or pages of a new kind of textbook, or they may be slides, or a series of slides or film loops projected on a screen for individual or group viewing, or tape-recorded words, passages, or music.

Various patterns for the development of sequences have been worked out, some of which have been briefly described by Glaser.[16] One of these is the so-called Ruleg system (*rule* plus *e.g.*, for example), according to which the frames first present a rule, principle or some other generalization, followed by

[16] In Coulson, *op. cit.,* pp. 67–85.

specific examples. More complex is the so-called lattice system [17] which is particularly valuable in developing the meaning of concepts. Along the baseline the programmer draws a series of squares and writes in them the names of the basic concepts needed in understanding the term, but which are already known to the student on entry into the program. Above these from left to right increasing in altitude like the side view of a low flight of steps another series of squares is plotted, containing the names of derived or constituent concepts in increasing order of complexity. This is the pedagogical lattice, the framework used to organize the sequence of learning materials which specifies the pattern of relationships. Thus the information is programmed for each square from the preceding and baseline squares so that the complex term whose meaning is sought, at the extreme upper right, is understood, with all needed connotations, in the light of all that has preceded.

Another plan for developing sequences of frames is the Mechner system, according to which the programmer writes on different colored cards the main points and the points subsumed under them. Quite different is a novel form referred to as redundancy programming, the principle of the sentence-completion scheme. It has been tried out in foreign language learning. In any prose passage some words are not strictly necessary, like *and* and *to* in the sentence, "The boys _____ girls went _____ the circus." But instead of blank spaces as in the usual programs, the foreign words are inserted, a few simple words at first, until the reader builds up quite a reading vocabulary on the basis of context. Still different is the spiral program

[17] Myron Woolman describes the process in the construction of a program in basic electricity in *Programming for Conceptual Understanding,* a report to the Communication Social Science Research Department of The Bell Telephone Laboratories. See also, Erwin H. Brinkmann, *Educability in Visualization of Objects in Space: A Programmed Instruction Approach,* Doctoral dissertation, University of Michigan, Ann Arbor (1963).

which covers a number of topics, say five or ten, at a very simple conceptual level, then circles around and covers the same topics at a somewhat more advanced level, building on what has gone before, and so on. This scheme has possibilities for building on related content from different fields as in general science or social studies.

How Should We Start?

Some schools are already equipped with teaching machines. People who have had experience with them always offer a word of warning phrased in various ways, all of which mean, "Don't start out in a big way!" It is better for a teacher first to find out what good programs are available in his area of interest. Then study the descriptions of machines on the market, and be sure the programs selected fit the machines. Plan where and when to use them, and don't buy more than needed. New models are constantly appearing. A number of references are already available,[18] but probably the best way is to participate in a workshop or university course devoted to an explanation of principles and to practice in programming.

Those who want to write their own programs should realize that this cannot be done in their spare time. Programming is a craft that is partly an art and partly a science. It is not the purpose here to introduce the various techniques in item construction—chaining, fading, prompts, lead-in, augmenting, reviewing, specifying, generalizing, and the rest. Nor is there space for an adequate discussion of the principles involved. Suffice it to say that programming is difficult, time-consuming, and therefore expensive. Counting the necessary try-outs and revisions one estimate is $1,000 for each hour of instruction. Another is one to two frames per man hour, or 150 to 175

[18] See bibliography references to David Cram, William J. Deterline, C. I. Foltz, David J. Klaus, Robert F. Mager, S. M. Markle, Wendell I, Smith, William Moore, and Lawrence M. Stolurow (especially Chaps. V and VI).

frames per man per month. About fifty frames are needed to cover the material of a one-hour lecture. Or, stated another way, it cost one industry $40 per hour, which it was believed could be reduced to $15 with practice. One program covering "one year of arithmetic" (whatever that is!) cost $50,000 to prepare.

So it is better to begin in a small way, on a restricted topic at first, with a subject matter specialist and a consultant to aid the half- or full-time programmer. Analyze the content in relation to the educational objectives, and program only the essential processes, what should be known and remembered, leaving to other media such parts as can be taught better in other ways; for example, geographical or historical background by films or books.

The production of programs is now in a state of flux. Engineering firms and publishing houses, as well as universities and other nonprofit organizations, are all getting into the act. More and more good programs are rapidly becoming available. The potential market not only includes public and private schools but also colleges and universities, industrial organizations, the armed services, and federal agencies, as well as similar organizations and institutions abroad, with programs ranging all the way from teaching illiterates to instruction in higher mathematics. It has been urged that programs which could be translated into foreign languages and shipped overseas have a distinct advantage over the export of teachers in that the programs are impersonal and uncontaminated with American cultural folkways.

Whether or not costs are reduced, there will be more education provided for the dollars spent, and the teaching will be improved. The potential market and the commercial interest added to the instructional possibilities make it safe to predict that teaching machines and programmed textbooks will eventually become an even more common feature in education and training than are paper-and-pencil tests today.

5

Systems and Organization

EDUCATIONAL OBJECTIVES are behavioral competencies to be habituated by means of various kinds of environmental control. In more primitive societies, a human being in the role of a teacher singlehandedly and without benefit of other resources was expected to provide the needed control of the environment. The procedure is suited to a limited range of activities and to a limited number of learners. The apprentice system, with instructional materials (the tools of the trade), continued the procedure as the practical arts developed. Beginners had to be taught to use tools, and gradually to operate machines. Tools and machines were improved so that they could be used or operated more conveniently, and they became increasingly efficient.

It is only natural that with rapid industrial growth would come technological changes in many human enterprises including education. Tools and machines have been used in controlling the environment of the learners, but largely as aids or adjuncts to the original medium, the teacher's voice. The earlier revolution that took place during the first decades of the present century was primarily psychological, social, and administrative, and changes along these lines are still going on.

But with the advent of television and self-instructional programs, new possibilities were opened up calling for a re-examination of the whole process in order to discover whether all the available media are being used together to the best advantage. As a consequence, it becomes clear that they are not, that a number of traditional practices in education have become obsolescent, and that in view of the increasing demands made on the schools, the equipment and operation of the educational plant are far from being as efficient as they might be.

The innovations are referred to loosely in various ways. Most general are the terms *medium, adjunct,* and *aid.* A medium is something or someone that stands between two other things, here between the learner and what is to be learned, hence a means. An adjunct, the term used by some to apply to the media, is merely something joined on to something else, but not necessarily a part, not fitted in to it. The term applies well enough to many of the ways the media are employed, but hardly a satisfactory arrangement. Aid carries the connotation of medium and adjunct, an auxiliary means hitched on—as a hearing aid or visual aid. This use, too, is unfortunate because it implies that a part of a process can properly be called an aid to that process, and raises the question as to what the process is as distinguished from its parts.

The means that are of a mechanical sort are referred to as tools, equipment, hardware, instruments, and gadgets. With the exception of the latter, which is colloquial and often deprecatory, each has a fairly well defined meaning. *Tool,* originally a hand-operated instrument, is often generalized to apply to any means. *Equipment* can refer to any movable, functional object, and *hardware,* to metal equipment to distinguish it from "software" such as baseballs and books. An *instrument* may or may not be hardware, is usually more complex than a tool, and, like it, is generalized to apply to any means. *Apparatus* is a complex instrument designed for some specific purpose. Interestingly enough, a machine etymologically is also a means (Greek *mēchanē* from *mēchos*). Nowadays it is hardware, made up of movable parts, thus more complex than a tool and capable of taking over some man-tool functions or others either impossible for man or possible only at greater cost in time and effort. Any of these devices may be teaching aids or media of instruction.

The last step seems to be *automation,* a new word from an ancient source. Like *automaton* and *automatic* it comes from *autos* plus the Sanscrit word *mata,* meaning *mind.* But the terms imply a self-sufficiency that the word *machine* does not, chiefly through the development of feedback and self-correctional devices. It is a far cry, however, from the safety valve and the thermostat to the digital computer, and whether or not either can "think" depends on one's definition of the term.

Systems

The question that faces educators today is not how any one of these instructional media can best be used in the schools as they now are, but rather, how they can best be fitted together, along with the school personnel, all to become not aids or adjuncts but components in an educational system. This is something more than training teachers to employ the new media— use the tools and operate the machines. The new technology requires that man learn to cooperate with the machines. He must know what each component can do, and so fit them into subsystems within the larger system.

A system has been defined in various ways. It is a complex, self-regulating, functional pattern of interrelated parts. It is a hierarchical series of sequential dependencies. It is "a set of components organized in a way that tends to constrain action toward a specific end." [1] It is any pattern of objects and humans that according to some plan or set of procedures, is required to perform a specific mission. An organism is a system, made up of a number of subsystems—digestive, circulatory, etc.—each with its input, feedback, and output operating more or less independently but functioning in harmony with other components and with the total system. Machines are not necessarily a part of a system, as in the term *social system,* or they may be implied as in *transportation system,* or dominant as in *weapons system.* When men and machines cooperate, the result is a man-machine system. Kennedy [2] has defined a man-machine system as "an organization whose components are men and machines, working together to achieve a common goal, and tied together by a communications network." Man's position in a man-machine system, besides designing it, is operating it. Stripped to its bare essentials, this consists of data transmission and processing. On the basis of his interpretation of observed data or "displays" (charts, gauges, instrument panel, etc.), he exerts certain controls over the total organization and its parts which transform inputs into outputs. He himself is thus one of the components.

"The allocation of teaching tasks to the instructor and the automated device may be regarded as a problem in assignment of function in a man-machine instructional system." [3]

Modern technology in education consists actually in studying the operation of the system and its components with a view to improving the operation of both. The human component— in education, teachers and other school personnel—as all are aware, requires considerable attention.

[1] John L. Finan, "The System Concept and Methodological Decision," in Gagné, *op. cit.,* p. 519.

[2] John L. Kennedy, "Psychology and Systems Development," in Gagné, *op. cit.,* p. 16.

[3] Meredith P. Crawford, "Concepts of Training," in Gagné, *op. cit.,* p. 338.

Kennedy [4] has outlined a series of decisions that are required in developing an efficient system. These will be recognized as familiar educational problems. First it must be decided whether or not a particular person should be acquired and made a component (selection). For this purpose screening devices are used—past record, tests, and interviews. Then it must be decided whether he should learn on the job or be put through some kind of training, or both, and if so what kind. For this purpose all available media (methods) for controlling the environment may be used that are appropriate and effective for different kinds of positions. Then the training experiences (curriculum) must be decided on and also the treatment of the individual—promotion, pay, and specific assignments.

But now it is necessary to go further and consider the design of the total system and of its component parts. Gagné [5] has outlined a series of steps or stages in systems development:

Statement of system purposes
Advanced operations design
Assignment of functions to man and machines
  Design stage including task description, task analysis, and job design
  Development state [including the decisions outlined above]
  Completing machine components and team teaching
  Testing
System training
System evaluation
Operational stage

Such a detailed procedure differs from the heuristic, trial-and-error and accidental-success methods by which innovations are often introduced into the schools, if they are introduced at all. Ideally the time to develop the design would

[4] John L. Kennedy in Gagné, *op. cit.*, p. 19.
[5] Gagné, *op. cit.*, p. 4.

be when a new building is planned. But unless the staff is ready for the change, the familiar *modus operandi* will continue in the new surroundings. The old Victorian furniture will be moved into the new modern apartment. Planning and training for the new ways is needed and fortunately this can, if necessary, go on in the old building.

TRADITION vs. SYSTEMS

Needed Revisions and Educational Objectives

As a first step it might be best to take another look at the educational objectives, however they may be formulated. Which policies and practices or what conditions interfere with their realization? A list might be drawn up of conditions that need remedying, including class size, promotion policy, reading instruction, equipment, teaching load, curriculum offerings, and so on. The usual procedure is to tinker with the most troublesome problem, such as overcrowding, and add a new wing, a new course, or a new teacher, or if the bond issue passed, even a new building, perhaps one that except for certain new building materials would have been a modern marvel in 1930. These may be good temporary solutions, but there is a danger that as a consequence things will not be much better than they were before.

Intrusion or Rationalization

Another procedure is to experiment with some new device like team teaching, television, or teaching machines (TT, TV, or TM). But there are right ways and wrong ways to do this. A number of schools, through the energy of their administrative officers, obtained language laboratory equipment which was delivered to the buildings when no one knew how to use it, and there were no plans for fitting it into the instructional program. MPATI beamed prepared lessons into the building under similar circumstances. Unless frantic efforts are made to rearrange schedules, provide the staff training needed, and develop instructional materials, the inchoate disruption may cause the efforts to be discontinued. Or at best, the results may be no better than under the old methods.

Some years ago the term *rationalization* was used to refer to streamlining the parts of an industrial enterprise into a system according to the principles of scientific management. The term is equally applicable to education. The intrusion of some new part in a dynamic structure may merely substitute for the old and have no appreciable effect, or, on the other hand, it may "gum the works" since the change may make all manner of other adjustments necessary. Instead, the whole structure needs to be studied and all the parts of the total process fitted together. Subsystems have to be developed within the total system. Finn delineated general administration, testing, and instruction as the three areas in which technology can be improved. Robert Miller early suggested the component parts of a man-machines system, and C. R. Carpenter showed their application to teaching and learning, while Stolurow recognized the need for greater efficiency and pointed to the consequent need for technological improvements, primarily in the use of automated devices and a systems approach to educational problems.

The Systems Approach

Following the rationalization idea, one might start where the school is and plan successive steps that must be taken in order to bring about the conditions sought. The planning would involve both equipment and personnel. The terms *input* and *output* are applied either to the performance of a single person or group, or to the operation of a machine or industrial system or complex that manufactures some product, like an automobile. But the input cannot be dumped in all at once. Various processes are involved requiring careful selection, variation, and timing. Different parts have to be applied in the proper amounts when they are needed.

Over the years educators have given a great deal of attention to this matter of process, including such problems as those of curriculum, method, evaluation, and promotion, but all efforts have been circumscribed by the assumption that the teacher-class subsystem is necessary. It has been taken as axiomatic that one teacher teaches a "course" or "grade," the content of which takes a year (or term) to complete, and that all the students should begin and end it together. Some of the greatest scientific discoveries have been made when investigators have dared to question an axiom. And if one follows their example and questions the validity of the teacher-class axiom, he soon realizes that it is actually more mechanical than the innovations that might supersede it. The method of assigning marks is an escape, a rationalization in the psychological sense of the term. It projects the failures of the system on the children and young people, giving low or failing marks to those who have not been properly classified or adequately taught, and at the same time giving rewarding marks to those who do well, some of whom may not even have needed the instruction.

In contrast, a systems approach [6] implies a careful study of the kind of treatment (input) required by each child, and the time when it is needed, in order to attain the objectives sought. "Systems analysis is the comparison of alternative means of carrying out some function, where the means are complicated and comprise a number of interrelated elements." [7] Educationally, it is making the best use of available resources within the framework of values that the school administrator has established or ascertained in the community. As has been

[6] See Gagné, *op. cit.;* also John F. Cogswell in *AID for Education and Training,* 5 (September, 1961), 43.

[7] James Mauch, "A Systems Analysis Approach to Education," *Phi Delta Kappan,* 43 (January, 1962), 158–162.

noted, the term *man-machine system* applies to the coordination of men and machines in producing a specific output. The machine simplifies or at least changes the performance of the man, although the over-all task remains the same. It is no longer merely the process of fitting tools to man's use, but of discovering what machines can do that man does with his tools, and what they cannot. Education has long employed a hesitant, piecemeal approach—one little innovation here and another there—without much conviction and without adequately fitting the pieces together into a total, unified process. All agree on the function of teaching as that of organizing the environment to guide learning activities toward the educational objectives. A man-machine system implies that if the means and responsibilities are realigned, the task can be performed more effectively. It implies further that the components can be so arranged that compatibility and purposeful performance are achieved by organization and readjustment among them.

If we concentrate on the task to be performed, a careful description and analysis are of primary importance, and consequent decisions on training procedures should be based on these and on the input conditions and on the output (objectives) sought.[8]

The main point in setting up such a system or combination of subsystems, as has been suggested, is that any change in any component must be analyzed and evaluated in relation to its effects on and interactions with all other components, and in relation to its effects on the operation and output of the total system. For example, the effectiveness of self-instructional devices, no matter how excellent in themselves, is dependent on interactions of different types of instruction, the roles played by school personnel, the scheduling of students, and so on.

[8] See Robert B. Miller in Glaser, *op. cit.*, Ch. 2, and in Gagné, *op. cit.*, Ch. 6.

If we concentrate on the personnel components of the system, the school staff, we realize that each member must fit into the whole structure in such a way that his peculiar contribution is made as effective as possible. This is why it is necessary to define the objectives of the system, and analyze the task and functions to be performed by the human components (the school personnel) and by the machines. Then the nature and extent of the output desired—new knowledge and skill and the behavior capabilities of the learner—must be specified. Personnel must be selected and trained to do what will be needed to contribute to the objectives of the system. With new and sometimes more specific tasks to perform, procedures for selection and training call for some modification.

Due care needs to be exercised in following through the stages in systems development listed by Gagné, above. Trial runs will probably be necessary, and these can sometimes be carried on experimentally in a simulated environment in which the several components can be tested, varied, and re-tested under fairly well-controlled conditions. Similarly, effective system performance may suggest the desirability of training personnel as a team under simulated conditions. This may be done by role-playing, an excellent simulator in social situations. Or "a school within a school" may be set up, involving, say, several different kinds of rooms and a control room, which will provide a feedback to improve the procedures and achieve an integrated performance.

But a systems approach necessarily involves some over-all design. Design in education has been defined by Robert W. Wagner [9] as "thoughtful artful organic use and creative control of necessary system." It is the reason why school "systems" should differ (though they may differ for less enviable reasons). Those who create them will order the parts in a

[9] Robert W. Wagner, "Design in Education," *The News Letter,* The Bureau of Educational Research and Service, Ohio State University, 27 (October, 1961), 1–4.

variety of ways according to the materials they use and their feeling for human values.

Technology, as has been noted, does not consist of machines alone, nor the personnel, nor is it the system, but it is the source and substance of them all. As stated earlier, the word literally means the science of construction. More specifically, it means applied science or science in support of the practical arts. Physics is basic to the engineering arts, biology to the medical, and psychology to the educational, although related sciences are also drawn upon. So rapid has been the industrial development of the last few years that many have come to think of technology as applying only to hardware. But this is too narrow a conception. As a matter of fact, many of the earlier inventions of the industrial age depended less on science than on a kind of common sense empiricism or a heuristic, problem-solving procedure. What looked like a good guess was tried out to see if it would work. More is now understood about the nature of the external world—the strength of metals and alloys, the permanence of dyes, the wearing qualities of building materials, tires, and textiles, and so on—so less guesswork is necessary. Similarly, education is becoming less dependent on folklore, tradition, and heuristic procedures, and more on the methods of science as they have been developed chiefly by psychologists in the area of learning, and social psychologists, in group processes. The points of view of the scientist and of the technologist are likely to differ in one interesting respect: the scientist is impressed with what we don't know, and the technologist with what we do. So the psychologically oriented writers are apt to point out the weaknesses and faults of television and of self-instructional programs, while the educationally oriented, if not hag-ridden by habit and tradition, are more apt to go ahead, make their programs, and try them out, or perhaps work out improvements in the process.

The true function of the technologist—whether industrial,

consulting, military or educational—is to employ psychology in a particular setting, that is, to the problems of one or another of the arts, to translate general laws and principles into specific operations of machines and people. As is well known, the contribution of science is threefold: knowledge and understanding of related natural phenomena; measurement and precision, hence more exact assessment; and method, including careful observation, repetition, record-keeping, control of variables, discovery of regularities, inference, and experimentation.

While these processes are not mutually exclusive, they roughly delineate the various activities employed by scientists in the quest for certainty. Technology is the scientifically-based activity involved in the development of the practical arts, in the making of new functional constructs, whether mechanical devices or organizations of people, or a combination of the two. In the latter, technology includes the design, organization, and operation of man-machine systems along the lines previously described.

Resources

No one at this time can give specific directions as to the best way for any one school to proceed in setting up a man-machine system for the improvement of learning and a closer approach to educational objectives. Some schools have already started with the introduction of one or another of the new media; and it is hoped that this is just a beginning, that the results obtained from this method of intrusion will not discourage the staff, and that efforts will be made to coordinate and integrate this medium and others as components and subsystems in a unified pattern of procedures. Other schools have done nothing as yet and may be considering what the first steps should be. In any case, it would seem that a logical approach would be to begin with the study of the available resources in money, equipment, and personnel. Within these limits, and before buying any machines, it might be desirable to study the possibility of developing an instructional materials center in one or more buildings.

Instructional Materials Center

A resources or instructional materials center provides the life blood of a man-machine educational system, and through it the developing technology finds its expression. It is the subsystem for information processing, not for administrative efficiency alone, but for promoting learning, the main function of the whole system. Fitts [10] has pointed to the need for a classification or taxonomy of information-processing tasks and suggests the following five chief categories:

Complete information processing—all the information can be covered in the response, as in typing, translating, playing music, and reading aloud.

Partial information processing—the needed information is selected or filtered off from what is not needed as in proofreading, censoring, withholding information.

Information reduction—the response, though a function of all the information, is reduced or condensed, as in summarizing, abstracting.

Algorithmic or heuristic problem solving—the stimulus content in the form of source information is transformed, either by following a set of rules (algorithmic), or by using the information in each step of a solution to aid in determining the next step (heuristic). This playing by ear, whether in personnel selection and assignment, or in developing a man-machine system, does not guarantee the optimum solution, but it is the best method available in many situations especially where there are several unknowns.

Decision making—the selection of a course of action on the basis of incomplete information or in the face of risk, like problem solving, is affected by feedback. Both will be operating at

[10] Paul M. Fitts, "Humans in Man-Machine Systems," *Research News,* The University of Michigan, 13 (July 1, 1962), 1–4.

all levels from decisions as to choice of resources to executive decisions as to policy, in small matters and in large.

Information processing thus runs the gamut of input-output discrepancy ranging from near zero to a pretty complete reorganization of the original. Presumably personnel data would be filed as confidential information; a resources or instructional materials center would be a place where all other information would be available. It would first of all be a place where printed material, audio-visual displays and equipment, a file of community resources, etc., are stored so that they are immediately available when needed. A California survey [11] employed the following categories for the organization and administration of instructional materials centers: procurement of materials, organization of materials within the center, dissemination of information to the staff, inventory operations, and responsibilities for professional and non-certificated personnel in relation to the objectives and functions of the center. The last item reveals that it is more than a dispensary. It is a place for reading, listening, and viewing by teachers and students, individually and in small groups, and where trained people can cooperate with other staff members and with students in helping to provide materials to satisfy their instructional and learning needs. One of its main functions is to help children and young people to become skillful and discriminating users of both printed and audio-visual material—the "partial information processing" of Fitts' taxonomy.

First to be considered would be the school library. Is there one? Is there a good one, or should there be additions to the list of books and resource publications it contains? Is the person in charge merely one who checks books in and out, or one who has had training as a school librarian? Is the library used

[11] Reported by Virginia C. Barnes, *The Organization and Administration of the Instructional Materials Center in Medium-Sized School Districts,* doctoral thesis (Stanford, Stanford University, 1960).

only as a study hall, or do students come to it for supplementary readings and in quest of source materials?

While inquiries and improvements are being made here, another committee can look in to the audio-visual set-up. As has been suggested, the situation in many schools is nothing less than deplorable. Cases have been reported where the budget is so badly planned that teachers have difficulty even in requisitioning a colored pencil! A little planning and a relatively small financial outlay would make the many kinds of audio-visual materials accessible and useful in the classroom. Perhaps most important, and corresponding to the trained librarian would be the trained audio-visualist who can make sound judgments about the purchase of equipment, keep it in working order, arrange a distribution system that will make the more cumbersome apparatus readily available, one who can serve as a consultant to other school personnel on films, slides, and other materials that can be made, rented, or bought, which will be helpful to them.

In the process of building up the library and audio-visual services into a coordinated resource center, questions will arise as to the points in the various school subjects where the different kinds of supplies can best be used, and whether provision might be made for a few kinescopes or teaching machines for certain children or for specific courses. Storage and accessibility of self-instructional programs are also to be considered. The possibilities of a language laboratory may be realized or television screens installed, or even a closed circuit TV camera. By this time a school is ready to plan its systems approach.

Some schools have begun with language laboratory equipment, with a shipment of teaching machines, or with television programs beamed in from outside. They may have the problem of bringing their library and audio-visual resources up to standard, and of tying them in with the new equipment. It is probably safe to say that the degree of success of a school in its technological transition will depend almost entirely on the ability of the administration to develop the organizational arrangements necessary, and on the ability of the staff to tolerate and even to welcome change. There is little chance that teachers will suffer from technological unemployment, but there will necessarily be a greater degree of role differentiation. This, however, is not new. As has been noted, we already have administrators, supervisors, visiting teachers, guidance workers, school psychologists, teachers of the handicapped, and others, to say nothing of subject matter specialists. Considerable satisfaction is derived from such specialization. Only the "classroom teacher" is the jack of all trades. His lot is not always a happy one owing to the many roles that he is called upon to play. A further careful differentiation of roles has every prospect of producing not only more effective learning, but also a higher level of job satisfaction.

Dean Francis S. Chase [12] of the School of Education of the University of Chicago, referring to an "accelerating change" in the years to come, noted the efforts to bring curriculum content more in line with new knowledge and the increased use of programming, television, and other audio-visual materials, and added what he referred to as the "search for new ways of allocating teacher responsibilities." Instead of trying to "reconstruct *the* teacher," we can better address ourselves to the question of the several responsibilities of school personnel.

ADMINISTRATORS

In considering the design for a man-machine system it is important to emphasize that man is still there, along with the machines, not only in person but also as the author of teaching machine programs and producer of television scripts. As has been noted, the phrase *technology in education* refers less

[12] As reported in *School and Society,* 89 (October 21, 1961), 331.

to machines as such than it does to the effective coordination of educational techniques and procedures for controlling the learning environment. Some have averred that the area of management in education is at least three decades behind industry. Data-processing equipment is beginning to find a place in the schools, while the possibilities of electronic scheduling, for example, are beginning to be explored. The machines, however, are not the whole story.

Administration

The administrator will have his usual responsibilities, but each will be somewhat different. The Educational Policies Commission [13] early called upon administrators to facilitate flexible scheduling, to provide adequate instructional facilities and resources, to select "communication conscious" and skillful teachers, and to stimulate staff in-service education in uses of the new media.

Public relations will require developing support for innovations. Organizing the curriculum and instruction will include more irregularities than now, and new sources. Staff utilization will present more complex problems in view of the differentiation of function, and will necessitate provision for more specialized training than at present; while planning and organizing learning resources, schedules, and work spaces will be an exacting task, but a rewarding one. The principal or superintendent will have the responsibility for making policy decisions and will have to work out the complicated arrangements for groups of different sizes meeting for periods of different lengths. Further they will be in charge of a more diversified staff than at present, staff assistants including clerks and technicians, staff specialists, and subject matter specialists.

[13] Cited by James W. Brown and John A. Moldstad in "Administration of Instructional Materials," *The Review of Educational Research, op. cit.,* p. 194.

It has been estimated that clerical and subprofessional tasks occupy about one-third of a teacher's time, and another third is taken up by work which could probably better be performed by various automated devices.[14]

Staff Assistants

A number of people on whole or part time will be employed some of whom will be education students receiving internship experience and training in the various staff functions. They will read and evaluate papers, reports, etc., confer with parents, supervise various projects, and participate under supervision in various staff activities, chiefly supervising or monitoring pupils on the playground, in the cafeteria, and auditorium, language laboratory, extra-class activities, hobby clubs, and so on. Business-trained clerks will perform their usual services and also take over preparing reports, scoring standardized tests, taking attendance, keeping records, and checking and distributing supplies. Technicians attached to the instructional materials center will be necessary to maintain the mechanical and electronic equipment.

Construction for the New Media

School buildings will have to be more flexible, so plant planning will be more difficult than heretofore. If a new building is contemplated, there will not only have to be cooperation with the architect, the school staff, the school board, and the community, as usual, but special consultants will be needed in planning for the new media.[15] The building should

---

[14] For a more detailed elaboration of possible structural changes, see J. Lloyd Trump and Dorsey Baynham, *Focus on Change—Guide to Better Schools* (Chicago, Rand McNally & Co., 1961).

[15] Amo DeBernardis, and others, *Planning Schools for the New Media,* Division of Education, Portland State College, Portland, Oregon, 1961; also, Harold D. Hauf, and others, *New Spaces for Learning,* School of Architecture, Rensselaer Polytechnic Institute, Troy, N.Y., 1961.

not be obsolete before it is completed. In addition to the matters that are now routine, such as ventilation, lighting, heating, playground space, etc., plans will include the following:

An instructional materials center to which, in one way or another, there is easy access from all parts of the building.

A language or sound laboratory with booths for recording and playback equipment, for teaching speech and languages, and for listening to music and other recorded productions, and with adequate arrangements for control and monitoring.

Electric outlets for radio and television, and conduits and raceways for the latter. Radio and television studios in larger schools.

Small-group areas for individual study, listening and viewing, and counseling and conferences.

Individual study space for students and also for teachers.

Medium-sized rooms with arrangements so that two or three can be opened up into a single large room.

Auditorium for lectures, dramatics, concerts, and other purposes but capable of being divided into two or three large rooms for various purposes.

Separate centers, laboratories, or workrooms for social sciences and area study, mathematics, natural sciences, vocational education and practical arts, and a gymnasium and playground for acquiring recreational skills.

Such, briefly, is the structure dictated by the modern educational technology for which administration will be responsible. In such a school there will be no grade rooms as such, but there will be home rooms usually for like-age groups. Students will go to appropriate laboratories, though the differentiation will be gradual in the early years. Because tasks will be adapted to student abilities, personal adjustment problems will be greatly reduced. They will therefore be taken out of the social studies program and placed where they belong, with the student personnel services to be handled according to need, individually or by group therapeutic techniques. Social studies at the junior high level can then become what it should be—the study of the social, intellectual, esthetic, economic, and political progress of man on this planet. Study in depth can be introduced through the separate social sciences in the senior high school and in college. Fascinating possibilities lie ahead in developing the necessary continuity in instruction which the use of the new media provides, unhampered by the strait jacket of traditional courses.

STAFF SPECIALISTS

Student Personnel Services

Besides the administrators and the subject matter specialists (whose functions will be discussed later), the modern technology will require more detailed and better coordinated student personnel services. The testing, diagnosing, advising, counseling, guidance, health, and home visitation functions have developed somewhat independently, and in many school systems are already being improved and unified. One of the by-products of the new media will be to force such modifications, since the impersonality of programmed and televised instruction, and adaptation to the differences among individuals, will require that more systematic attention be given to the needs of each. The pupils will be expected to receive instruction each according to his abilities, so that one may be achieving, say, at what is now referred to as the "fourth-grade level" in arithmetic, "fifth-grade" in reading, and "sixth-grade" in science. His competence in different areas will be assessed, and in each he will work at his own level and at his own rate. The time when his competence will be recorded on punched cards and his classification determined by a computer may not be so far off as we think. But the holes in the cards will be the consequence of careful individual and group tests administered and interpreted by experts. School psychologists are now being trained in this function, but many tests are inadequate and new ones will have to be constructed. Even with good tests, much of the school testing is presently of questionable value since the children are usually placed together in the same grades or classes they would have been in anyway. With the new media, testing will make it possible not only to "understand the child," but also to do something definite with the test results.

As programs are developed, the feedback to the school psychologists will provide additional data for either reclassifying the pupils or improving the programs; and for the former, as well as for the usual personality adjustments, the advising, counseling, and guidance functions will need to be improved. It is probable that a large block of undesirable school behavior will be eliminated as the students find themselves faced with tasks at their own levels of ability, neither so easy as to be a bore, nor so difficult as to produce excessive frustration with the consequent apathy, anxiety, aggression, or hostility.

Examination and Appraisal

It is not too much to hope that the development of educational technology will provide the occasion for abolishing the present procedures for marking and reporting to parents. The method of invidious comparisons of children who by law or chance find themselves together in the same classroom or course, comparisons derived from a combination of inadequate measurement and personal prejudice [16] and condensed into a single symbol, constitutes about as irrational procedure as could be conceived by so-called rational human beings.

For each of the different areas of skill and knowledge a continuous line of increasing competence could well be drawn, say from zero for complete ignorance to 1000 for

[16] As this was being written the newspapers reported the case of a boy who was failed in all his subjects, in which his work was satisfactory, because of his duck-tail haircut.

perfection, and people could be tested and scored along this line whatever their grade or age. Thus one's competence in French or algebra or swimming would be measured not in comparison with others in the chance agglomeration of abilities that happen to be found in any one grade, but on the basis of his absolute ability. An individual's competence in any one area would be, say, 47, 226, or 659. (Constituent skills could of course be measured separately, like pronunciation and comprehension in a foreign language as suggested earlier.) That this has not been done long ago is no doubt due to a lack of satisfactory units of measurement comparable with time or distance units in track, for example. Such units make it ridiculous to talk about seventh-grade running ability, for example, or college broad jumping, as we now refer to seventh-grade French or college algebra. Without measuring units, however, a school orchestra is made up of those who can play well enough to be in it, whatever grade they may be in. There seems no reason why the same cannot be done with varying degrees of exactitude, to be sure, in other areas.

But people have become so enamored of the customary age and grade averages which are used as norms [17] and the standard deviations and probability curves, that any other way of thinking is most difficult. Since it might be unkind to deprive the statistically minded of their familiar concepts, it should be pointed out that when the linear scales have been devised, there will be plenty of opportunity to find the distributions of all kinds of groups on them, not only those in the same grade (where there are grades), but of the same age, and for those having had periods of instruction of different lengths when various media are employed.

For example, if desired, a positive or negative standard score could be used to show whether among twelve-year-olds,

[17] For a criticism of grade norms, see L. J. Cronbach, *Essentials of Psychological Testing* (New York, Harper & Row, Publishers, 1960), pp. 385–388.

in a particular ability, a child is accelerated or retarded. While such scores for an individual might indicate the desirability of a study of wide deviations, they would not imply that his performance should be brought up to (or kept down to) the average. In some cases an arbitrary cutting point might be used as a standard of sufficient proficiency for academic or vocational purposes, just as number of words per minute is a criterion for typists and stenographers.

In any case, what is commonly referred to as "remediation" will tend to disappear and be replaced by adequate instruction continuing from the start. The need for remedial work came as a consequence of promotion policies which placed children in grades where some of the tasks required of them were beyond their abilities, and instruction was not adapted to their needs. True, if a child has acquired wrong habits, corrective instruction may be required to change them, and this may demand more individual instruction than would have been needed to teach right habits in the first place. If instruction in each subject or skill starts where the pupil is and proceeds at a rate determined by his own native ability and rate of growth, and he is allowed to progress as if the school system were set up for him alone, there will be little need for remediation. New measuring instruments and the new media bring this ideal within the realm of feasibility.

Sam M. Lambert, director of the research division of the National Education Association, in an AP news release, stated that the upper 15 to 20 per cent of ninth graders could complete their high school work in three years instead of four, and that probably 5 per cent of the first graders are bright enough to finish the 12 grades in 10 or 11 years, while intensive remedial [18] reading work for lagging students would

---

[18] The use of *remedial* here is an interesting illustration of the influence of old speech habits even among the frontier thinkers. More appropriate for "intensive remedial reading work" would be the single word *coaching*, or intensive instruction in reading.

enable them to finish high school in 12 years instead of 13 or 14 or even 15. Lambert saw a considerable saving in tax dollars in this, although his plan called for summer instruction and a six-year minimum teacher-training program for all teachers, which would undoubtedly use up some of the savings. Pupils for whom reading or any school task proved unusually difficult will be referred to psychologists for examination to determine the causes of the difficulty, and to persons especially trained to teach them. Special education will thus assume greater importance than it does at present in most schools, as a liaison between the student personnel services and the regular instructional program. Or, putting it another way, all education will be special education that is adapted to the weaknesses and strengths of all the pupils.

Homeroom Teachers

In the elementary school grade room the child now finds his in-group to which he belongs and in which he can find security and friendship. Usually in the departmentalized secondary school a brief homeroom period serves a similar function. With individualized instruction made possible by the new media, it is especially important not to neglect the means of continuing personal contact among pupils and staff which the homeroom provides, although it might assume one or another of a number of different forms. It might take a half an hour more or less, and activities might range from business meetings to individual study. Its chief function, however, will be to assist in the individual and social adjustment of its members.

Each homeroom might be made up of children of the same age. Thus those who entered the first grade in the same year would make up the same homeroom as long as they remain in school, though they would go to different laboratories at different times according to their respective interests and abilities. Or homerooms could be made up of children of different ages. Experiments with ungraded classes have shown that we-feeling is developed in such groups as in a family. The older tend to look out for the younger, and the younger learn from the older. Since they are not competing with each other for marks, children develop quite friendly attitudes.

Those who are at about the same level of ability, say in reading or some other subject, might be in the same room although they would go their separate ways for other subjects or activities. A variation of this plan would be to have the pupils who seem to have special talent in a certain subject share the homeroom of a teacher of that subject who would serve as their adviser. The homeroom teacher's function will become professionalized, requiring specialization in personality theory and group therapy, counseling and guidance. A combination of these methods, described by George D. Stoddard,[19] is to be found in his so-called "dual progress plan," supported experimentally by the Ford Foundation. Following this plan, the homeroom teacher adds reading and social studies to the counseling responsibilities for alternate morning and afternoon grade groups, while on the other half days the same children are taught by specialists in other subjects, in which pupils progress at their individual rates. While this plan presents one excellent workable scheme to break the strangle hold of the self-contained classroom, individualization in *all* subjects with the aid of programmed instruction would seem to be a desirable next step.

Another plan would be for the homeroom teacher to be in charge of several homerooms successively throughout the school day, the students in them would constitute his case load, and he would be the custodian of their records. Or he might have fewer rooms in his charge and give part time to individual counseling. But he would be wholly relieved, if he so desired, of any additional instructional responsibilities.

[19] George D. Stoddard, *The Dual Progress Plan* (New York, Harper & Row, Publishers, 1961).

Some homeroom teachers might give part time to home visitation, if properly trained to do so, though others might serve full time in this capacity. The home visitors, now in some states called visiting teachers, are the staff social workers. It will be their function, not only through home visits but also through parent conferences, to maintain liaison with the parents, interpreting the school program to them and enlisting their cooperation in matters of adult-child relationships. It is well known that even a glimpse at parents or at home surroundings often does much to explain child behavior and to suggest directions for treatment. Members of the pupil-personnel staff, including homeroom teachers and regular counselors, whatever the organizational pattern, will be available to other staff members for conference in order to give them information about children and assist them in providing the kind of environmental control that is as nearly perfect as possible for each child.

Research—Evaluation and Development

In addition to better coordinated student personnel services there will be a research service for evaluation and development. This aspect of the school program is too often neglected, and as a consequence there is no adequate feedback on the operation. In fact, until teaching machines appeared and were forced to defend themselves, relatively little attention was given to the extent to which the schools were actually meeting their announced objectives. For example, it has been contended that machine programs could not teach pupils to be creative, but few had thought to ask whether the traditional procedures had this effect. Now the objectives are becoming more sharply defined. The purchase of added equipment must be justified, and the customary marks or even scores on standardized tests are not sufficient. The schools can no longer rationalize their failures by projecting them on home background and mental depravity. They will be required to do more than merely keep young people off the streets and out of the labor market. They must show results. This is entirely fair and reasonable. And not only will appropriate research point to present weaknesses and suggest further improvement, but it should also be expected to bring to light new knowledge about the learning processes.

SUBJECT MATTER SPECIALISTS

For some time, change has been in the direction of greater specialization not only in education but in other occupational categories as well. The period of the generalist was in many ways an interesting and pleasant one, but the life was often disappointing because the generalist simply did not know enough about the different things he was supposed to do. In medicine the mistakes were tragic, but now, though there are general practitioners, there are increasing numbers of specialists—bone and joint, heart, internal medicine, and so on. A patient is now not merely given the dubious assurance that the doctor is doing "the best he can," but that his treatment is all that medical science can provide. In agriculture, there are still farmers, but there are also dairy farmers, poultry farmers, fruit farmers, and the rest. In dentistry there are those who specialize in extracting, inlays, prothesis, and orthodontia. Similarly in other occupations responsibilities have been divided. In education we have those trained for teaching different age groups, different handicaps, different subjects, and others, like librarians, curriculum coordinators, and supervisors. Just as the functions of those dealing with student personnel problems need to be clarified and rationalized (in the industrial sense) so do those related more directly to instruction.

Technology is now forcing the changes. Teachers' roles, as we have seen, require a preposterous array of competencies.

And while there will always be teachers, as there are doctors and farmers, a greater degree of specialization should result in a higher level of performance and greater individual satisfaction. No one knows how the differentiation of function will proceed. But if it is possible to project what is now going on into the future, as was done for the staff specialists, the result may be something like what is described below, although considerable variation is to be expected.

Learning Materials Consultants

In many places the school librarian holds a well-established position and performs an extremely useful function. In other places there is a long way to go before the library plays the part it might in the intellectual and cultural life of the school. Programmed learning, if it is to serve its proper function, will lead the student to competent independent inquiry carried on through library resources. The school librarian is not only a kind of museum curator, a custodian of books, but he is a professional educator who is a materials specialist familiar with various printed learning resources, and who can make appropriate selections from these, evaluating them for educational purposes. He is a consultant both with students and with teachers.

Audio-visual materials in general are much less satisfactorily housed than books, and much less effective in instruction than they might be. The audio-visualist should be more in demand as one who is expected to promote an improved educational program. He does not just run a hardware store, nor is he merely an authority on the care and treatment of gadgets. He has been thought of in the role of a learning technologist who is essentially an innovator, and as a supervisor of instructional resources. He will be a professional educator who understands the teaching-learning processes, and is familiar with the sources of materials and of their possible use in connection with the various school subjects. The formula for the materials consultants at present seems to be to acquire needed materials, to house and organize them in ways that will make them most easily accessible, and to distribute them so as most effectively to enrich the learning environment.

Programmers

In some ways, the use of the word *program* and its derivatives, borrowed from the computer jargon, is unfortunate, and perhaps a special word like *prolog,* for instance, would have been better. As things now are, *program* refers to the directions fed to a computer, a TV schedule, and a curriculum plan, as well as to what they hand you in the theater. But unless otherwise specified, in educational writing it refers to the materials earlier described that are fed into teaching machines or printed in scrambled textbooks of one kind or another.

Teaching machines have been likened to books with blank pages. They are the vehicle of instruction, or the packaging. While this takes some doing, it is nothing without the content. Programs in different subject matter areas are being produced commercially, and the business is developing at a rapid rate. The quality of the programs varies and will vary as does that of published books. But teachers ask whether they too, should not write programs, at least for special courses or particular student groups, for areas not yet provided for, or for specific parts of courses that can clearly be taught by this medium. In spite of the difficulty and cost of programming, it seems reasonable that home-made programs will be used. Those who are peculiarly adept will no doubt be called into commercial firms, especially if they are competent in the subject matter area. And in the schools, they will be needed not only to construct programs to some extent but also to assist in the choice of those to be purchased, and to make the revisions, the need for which they will probably discover as a consequence of using them.

Monitors

People are needed in the language laboratory, at the console, and/or in a separate room to monitor the students' language-learning efforts. Thus a new kind of teacher may be expected, one who sits with earphones listening in on one circuit or another, providing correction and reinforcement to learners he may not see. But monitoring will be a broader function than this. While the teaching machine or programmed textbook provides the correct answers, the feedback on mistakes will reveal student variation calling for reclassifying, perhaps for branching programs, and involving extra drill and special instruction, or in some cases referral to the student personnel services. Similarly, stand-by instructors will be needed for television and film presentation who will determine their teaching effectiveness perhaps by oral or written questions or give explanations to supplement the presentations. When television first appeared, the "regular teacher" was also present, partly to learn, and partly because schools were divided into rooms, grades, and courses. In the future this kind of featherbedding will probably disappear. The students will be of different ages, from different homerooms, and will meet with a monitor perhaps in an auditorium or oversized classroom, while for the next television showings in a different subject a quite different group will assemble.

Then too, some kind of monitoring will be necessary for teaching machines to see that students get the right programs, and that the machines are in order. For both television and teaching machines the monitor may become a kind of combination of floor manager to keep things running smoothly, and morale officer providing security and personal friendliness. He will perform a very important function. Unless he is part-time programmer for feedback evaluation he need not be an expert in the subject he is monitoring (as the language monitor must be), but he must know children both from books and experience, and he must know his machines.

Demonstrators

Educational television calls for special talent, often referred to as a "gifted teacher," to serve as lecture demonstrator. The cameras are usually on him as he talks, points to his charts and diagrams, or presents his demonstrations. If the content takes over from time to time, as is to be expected when the potentialities of the medium come to be more and more realized, he continues as narrator. His message is, "This is how it is; let me show you." There are many so-called gifted teachers who are quite hopeless at this kind of thing. Their gifts lie in other directions, sometimes in personal charm and the ability to get quite a bit of mileage out of a relatively small fund of information. Ideally the demonstrator is an unusual combination of scholarship and histrionics, and is likely to become the kingpin or queen bee of the faculty, commanding and deserving a higher salary than some of the others. He cannot hide in his classroom and close the door. He is on view where all may see. If disgruntled colleagues object to the salary differential, they can be given a screen test. If they are really as good as they think they are, they will no doubt become lecture demonstrators, for such talent will be sought and rewarded. But they must be able to do more than put on a good show; they must be able to teach.

Directors

There are some kinds of instructional situations for which, at present at least, machines seem not to be fitted, namely those which necessarily involve person-to-person relationships. One area is the acquisition of interpersonal skills in athletics, music, and dramatics, for which a coach, conductor, or director is needed. Already filmstrips and loops are in use to assist the learner in individual athletic skills ranging from throwing a baseball or serving in tennis to fancy diving. Film-strips with accompanying recorded directions, which have been called audiovismatic devices, provide the step-by-step teaching of hand skills. These can no doubt be developed to provide much of the routine beginning instruction in skill and strategy. In team sports, however, the learner must leave his chair beside the machine, put on a suit, and get out on the floor or the field. Here the coach may merely toss in the ball and pay little attention to what goes on, but preferably he will instruct the players as to what to do under varying circumstances and then give them practice in doing it. Their progressive approximations will be reinforced and their proficiency increased.

Similarly in ensemble playing and dramatics, basic skills in the production of tone, in technique, enunciation, and so on can presumably be aided by the development of auto-instructional devices. But the production of a balanced performance requires that the participants practice together under trained direction.

Discussion Leaders

A second area where learning in interpersonal situations is necessary and very important is in group discussion and planning. Student discussions, particularly in social studies, but also in other subjects, have been regarded by some as futile, since in trying to bring out the ideas of the students the teacher regretfully discovers that they are sadly lacking in one necessary ingredient, namely, a knowledge of any facts. The situation is changed when they have all previously acquired some of the facts, as is possible with programmed instruction, and the task is that of balancing, weighing, and reorganizing them. Of course, good discussion leads to the quest for more facts, but there is no need to start with the fairly common practice of sharing ignorance. In foreign language classes discussion can be carried on in the language being learned. In mathematics and science different solutions to problems can be discussed in much the same way a high-level science team works on a project.

The consideration of suggestions and criticism of ideas, plans, and policies, with their possible consequences becomes much more interesting and profitable. One college professor remarked that in his opinion no form of machine or programmed learning can take the place of the seminar, and he was right. For members of a seminar have presumably built up a background of knowledge about whatever problem they are discussing, and the value of the give and take among informed people led by a scholar in a particular field is beyond question.

Discussion leaders probably require as great or greater depth and breadth of scholarship and as much perceptiveness as do television lecture demonstrators. They, too, should and probably will be among the aristocrats of the profession. Not everyone can lead a discussion, involve the diffident, stimulate rational thinking, and give practice in group decision-making, which is so much a part of our modern culture with its numerous committees, boards, conferences, commissions, and the rest. The possible long-range value of group discussion should not be underestimated. The habits and insights students may acquire, what they learn from the leader and from each other, although it is not always possible to identify clearly, is applicable in the hundreds of small groups to which they will later belong which determine policy and its implementation. And in such groups ideas are born and nurtured which, when matured, will affect not only the life and happiness of the individual and his organization but also the wider public, and in rare cases the destiny of nations.

THE ORGANIZATION

Such staff functions as those described above will be performed by people. The schools cannot and will not be dehumanized by the introduction of better technology. Quite the reverse. All staff members are teachers in the broad meaning of the word, although they do not all do the same things. Since this is the case, it will be well to get rid of the stereotype, at least so far as is possible. We can make the effort to speak no more of the function or role of *the* teacher, the personality of *the* teacher, or even the perceptions, self or otherwise, of *the* teacher. School personnel functions will differ widely as will personality requirements and perceptions.

Any one staff member may have just one of the roles described, or because of special talents or the exigencies of the circumstances in a particular school system, and in accord with his training, he may act in dual or multiple roles. The function of each is to manage that part of the school environment for which he is responsible, so that the best educational experience is provided for each student, who will progress through its increasing complexities at the rate that is suited to his needs and abilities.

6

How It Might Work

IN THE PREVIOUS CHAPTER some of the components that would be used in a systems approach in education were examined. It remains to consider how they might look in operation. To do this, the author arranged a visit to a couple of imaginary schools that have broken through the tradition barrier and emerged in running order on the other side. It was thought that such a view might bring the different facets of the technological goal sought into clearer perspective and it might then be easier to devise ways of reaching them, although the routes taken by different people will not necessarily be the same. But first, a summary of some of the important preparatory steps that must be taken to avoid making a mess of things, which it is quite easy to do.

PLANNING FOR CHANGE

Stages

The first stage would be that of orientation. Some well-informed person might be asked to talk to the teachers and answer questions about the new media. Published material, of which there is now a considerable amount (see bibliography), and more appearing every day, can be obtained and studied, with faculty discussion of the possibilities. Teachers can suggest ways in which changes might be introduced into the grades and courses they teach. Sample equipment can be procured and tried out in rooms where teachers are most interested. If electronic equipment is to be purchased and installed, it is important not to be penny wise and pound foolish. One can save money on television apparatus and as a result get nothing but snow on the screen.

The second preparatory stage would consist of planning in relation to budget and space considerations and educational objectives, and where the greatest needs lie. All this might take a year or two, perhaps longer. It might be decided to start, not with the new media at all, but by building an instructional materials center and organizing the student personnel services. If the language departments are anxious to set up a language laboratory, if they have not done so already, this should perhaps follow. But if they still believe that grammar is of first importance the time is not ripe. Perhaps by this time the Carnegie unit requirement will have been modified so that arrangements could be made for continuity of language instruction. Conversation classes as now found in many elementary schools would probably be a desirable innovation, but not if that is where language instruction stops.

If the preliminary stages of orientation, planning, and tryout are satisfactorily taken, a school should be ready for transition to the revised system. This will have to be carefully planned and rehearsed by the staff before school opens.

Staff Preparation

In the matter of staff preparation one may as well be realistic. Some teachers think that when a principal or superintendent wishes to introduce innovations, he merely wants to make a reputation for himself. And some administrators view creative suggestions of teachers as a nuisance that is upsetting to a smooth-running organization: "When you have been in the profession as long as I have, . . ." and the enthusiastic teacher shudders at the thought and retires defeated. But in the thousands of schools where enthusiasms are shared, and where mutual trust and respect prevail, where there is a genuine *esprit de corps,* things can move. Financial and other arrangements can be made for staff training in workshops or courses, either on the ground or on a university campus, or both.

Public Information

All this activity cannot go on in a vacuum. The community will need to be brought in by the usual means, including parent meetings, news items, and telecasts. In view of the parental resistance to revisions of report cards alone, the difficulties of the public-relations task should not be underestimated.

THE ELEMENTARY SCHOOL

As we [1] approached the imaginary school of the future with its new educational technology we observed that in outward appearance it was not much different from a good modern school plant of the 1950's. We noted the same low building set in a well-kept lawn, the parking area with its school buses, the playgrounds, and, of course, above the roof, the television antennas. Inside, the differences did not become evident at once.

---

[1] For these imaginary visits the editorial "we" is used. It should be realized, however, that each of the innovations found is already in operation somewhere. See Arthur D. Morse, *Schools of Tomorrow— TODAY.* What remains is to incorporate each as a component in a system.

The Homeroom

Our guide, who introduced herself as a homeroom teacher, led us first to a room where small children were engaged in the usual rhythms and games.

"I suppose this is the first grade?" we innocently inquired.

"This is an ungraded school," she replied, apparently oblivious of our discomfiture, "so such rooms as these are homerooms, not grade rooms, but all the children in this room entered school for the first time last fall." As we choked back the impulse to retort, "Well, what's the difference!" or something of the sort, she went on blandly, "At the start, the children spend practically all their school time together in their homerooms. A few can already read when they come, while others will not be able to for two or three years. They are all tested and each is started on the programmed lessons suited to his ability."

Programmed Learning

In the next room we entered, a number of children were using teaching machines which we noted were of different kinds. Some were pressing their fingers on a transparent panel under which various diagrams and pictures successively appeared; the pressure brought the next diagram into view. Others were pushing buttons beside short sentences. "In this way," our guide was saying, "the brighter children rapidly cover the early simple materials; others have weeks of prereading experience before they are ready."

"But doesn't this mean that by the end of the first year some of the children will be doing second-grade reading?" we asked, and hastily added, "second-year reading."

"You are learning fast," our guide smiled. "Actually we do not like the term 'ungraded school.' It suggests that something is wrong or incomplete, like unpainted or unbuttoned. We prefer continuous-progress or continuity school. Under the old pattern in many schools, the first-grade teacher tried to get all the pupils through the first-grade readers, which was impossible for many of them. Some were failed and made to repeat, some were grudgingly passed and took up their position at the tail of the line. The brighter ones had to be slowed down, because they couldn't begin the second-grade readers until they got into the second grade, where the next teacher took over. Next year all will continue in their homeroom together, but each will take up his reading instruction where he leaves off this year."

"Does this mean that all cover the same programs but at different rates?" we asked.

"Many of them do," our guide explained. But there are certain check points where if a pupil has difficulty he is branched off to programs and primers that give him more practice in what has been covered. In a slow track, there might be 500 frames and in a fast track only 300 between the same two check points.

Personal Attention

"Sometimes," our guide continued, "one or more of the children seem to make no progress at some point of difficulty, so they are given individual attention by the monitor, who is a kind of expert tutor. She diagnoses their difficulties and gives them personal help when they need it, instead of allowing them to practice their mistakes—or skip them, which was the procedure during the vogue for remedial reading. The difficulty may be due to some misunderstanding on their part, to some undetected speech, hearing, or visual defect or it may lie deeper, in which case the pupil is referred to the psychological services."

While our guide had been talking, the children who had been at the machines had left them, and their places were taken by the other half of the homeroom group who had been listening to a story being read to them by the homeroom supervisor. With the help of the monitor the children obtained their programs and soon the buttons were being pushed again. This time, the programs looked more mathematical. As we moved on into another homeroom where the children were older, we asked our guide what would happen if a child were capable of doing fourth-year work in arithmetic but only third-year or second-year work in reading. She smiled at our efforts. "You see," she explained, "it really makes no difference whether or not one merely avoids the word 'grade.' We have finally realized that there is no such thing as third-grade or third-year work. It is what the psychologists call a fiction, the part of the traditional curriculum that children of average ability were expected to be able to do. Actually, all we have is work that is increasingly complex. Any one child might be doing more advanced work in one subject than in another, and this applies throughout the whole school. So we find it more satisfactory to provide instruction at the level of his abilities than to try to classify him in some grade or other."

Discussion

By this time we had passed a couple of larger rooms, one where a motion picture film was being shown, and the other where the children were intently watching a large television screen. "At some of the check points I spoke of," our guide continued, "and these are found in all programs and at all levels, a new start is made. The children who take up a new country in geography or a new process in arithmetic, or anything like that, are taken off the machines. Some are shown review films, illustrations, or applications on television, or given an introductory orientation to what is coming next. Or they may go to one of the conference rooms for discussion and questions with the discussion leader, where they can talk about what they have been learning. Sometimes they dramatize what they have learned or work up projects of one sort or another. This is the time for questions or criticisms or for any original ideas they may have."

Perceptual Content

"Other films or television programs give an orientation in what is to come. They provide what we call perceptual control. Television, in particular, gives excellent demonstrations and explanations, some by our own teachers, and the pictures help bring the words to life."

We stopped for a few moments to hear a spirited discussion, which ranged from the national parks to the bottom of the Indian Ocean. "Do the children get all this information from teaching machines and TV?" we asked. "Isn't there still a place for books?"

"Books seem to be more important than ever," our guide replied. "Before referring to specific books or periodicals, either in machine or television programs, we have to be sure copies are available in the library. For some reason the pupils are more alert than they used to be. There is often a rush of fifteen or twenty of them to the library as soon as the program is over."

"We are now coming to the instructional materials center," our guide continued. We noted that some pupils were reading, as in any library, others were working together in alcoves, while still others in soundproof rooms were listening to recordings or following intently the successive steps in the use of different tools as illustrated on a slide projector with the accompanying oral directions on tape. Beyond were staff offices, a workroom, and storerooms for films, tapes, and kinescopes, and for projection apparatus.

"We are particularly fortunate in our librarian and audiovisualist," our guide remarked, indicating two people at a table in a small room behind a glass door. "They work as a team and help us find materials we can use, sometimes things we had never heard of before."

Research

"Do you have regular team teaching here?" we asked.

"Yes, but not for the younger children," she answered, "and we are experimenting with it for the older. It certainly served a good purpose in helping to break up the self-contained classroom, but with our present personnel organization it does not seem so necessary. What we find is that other kinds of staff teams seem to form themselves to deal with common problems, especially homeroom supervisors, and monitors. A graduate student from the University is making a study of what he calls spontaneous team formation and the roles of their members. He hopes to use it for his doctoral dissertation."

"Are there other studies going on?" we inquired.

"Oh yes," was the reply. "There is one on the use of teaching machine programming in connection with television lessons that I happen to know about, and another on the use of the new media for the mentally handicapped, and there are several others."

On the way out we glanced in at a practice session of the school orchestra, and at a rehearsal of a little play in which fairies had penetrated into the technological age. "We have more time for things like these than in the old days," our guide remarked. "I like to call them the things of the spirit."

She bade us goodbye, and as we went down the walk, we were thinking that much we had observed could be found in any good school. The innovations had all been tried out separately before. But the difference was that here they were working together. This smooth-running job was the man-machine system we had read about. We could not say that the children's eyes were agleam, or that their faces shone with a new light. Indeed, they looked very much like children everywhere, some serious, some gay, all going about their various tasks. But we suddenly realized that in all the time we had been in the school, we had not seen any child scolded or reprimanded, which was perhaps not unusual. But the cordiality and friendliness of children and staff showed it was a happy ship. There was something that we still could not lay our finger on. We got into our car and pressed the starter, and then it came over us. It makes sense, and it works! That was it. Would we feel the same way about the high school?

THE SECONDARY SCHOOL

Few high school graduates know how to study independently or how to participate effectively in group tasks. Two-thirds of the professional high school teacher's time is wasted on tasks that could be done as well or better by others or by automated devices. The rigid curriculum units are irrational and illogical, and school houses are not suited to educational purposes. These statements are not quoted from a letter to the editor by "Disgruntled Taxpayers." They are some of the conclusions from five years' work of the Commission on Experimental Study of the Utilization of Staff in the Secondary School, as reported in 1961.[2]

James D. Finn [3] emphasized the desirability of combining the technology of individual and mass instruction with conventional methods and cited as a model for such a system the program developed by the Physical Science Study Committee at the Massachusetts Institute of Technology. It involved a revised textbook, the use of paperback supplementary books, a laboratory manual, a manual on how to build certain apparatus, some finished apparatus, about eighty motion pictures and other audio-visual material, and a teachers' manual. The authors described what they called a series of black boxes, the idea being that one or more of the boxes can be

[2] Trump and Baynham, *op. cit.*
[3] James D. Finn, *Teacher Education—Direction for the Sixties,* Tenth Biennial Survey for Executives, Bemidji State College, 1961.

used to create a system which would attain the desired objectives of any instructional task. The labels on the boxes were *mass presentation, individual automated teaching, human interaction, individual study,* and *creative activity.* The anomaly is that while the critics have accused educators of overemphasizing methods to the exclusion of content, the reverse has actually been the case. The child, his growth and development, and his attitudes and social background have been studied, which is all to the good, but methods have been neglected. Surely a visit to a high school of the future should be an enlightening experience.

The School Plant

The principal, who served as our guide to the imaginary high school we visited next, was a bundle of energy and enthusiasm. "Yes," he said, as he piloted us about, "it would have sounded crazy a few years ago, but we have finally succeeded in developing a high school without classrooms. That doesn't mean that students don't meet in groups, or that they are not taught by what used to be referred to as 'the living teacher.' I always liked that. We certainly haven't tried any dead ones! But it does mean that the students taking biology or algebra or German, or any other subject, do not go to the same room every day for fifty minutes and listen to the same teacher try to cover the same amount of work, whether or not the students do.

"Our problem," he went on, "is a little different from what they have in the elementary school because here the boys and girls are older and can take care of themselves. The schedule is laid out for each as a consequence of their earlier progress on their programmed instruction, and of course on the basis of their abilities as shown by tests, and their academic and vocational objectives."

What we saw was in some ways a duplication of what we had observed in the elementary school except that it was on a larger scale. The egg-crate, multiple classroom construction has been abandoned in favor of centers—the laboratory or workroom type of organization. The instructional materials center, like the one in the elementary school, was the center or core of the building complex. Around a large library reading room were numbers of smaller rooms. At one end students were working in individual study spaces, some with books, others with teaching machines. Through glass doors one might observe students in individual and group listening stations making use of records and tape recorders. In similar rooms which served as small-group conference areas, ten or fifteen students (sometimes with a teacher) were gathered around a central table and looked as if they were planning projects of some sort. In other rooms students were viewing films and using microfilm readers. Our guide showed us how these rooms were arranged in pairs, those in each pair being separated by retractable partitions. To the rear were areas for equipment storage and for audio-visual materials production, the latter a busy workshop where students and learning-materials consultants were engaged in preparing posters, slides, and photograph enlargements. In a large alcove was the technicians' instrument maintenance and service area.

At the other corner, students filled the booths of the language laboratory, and beyond this was the speech and drama production studio which apparently doubled for television, since at that moment the lights were on, the camera was in place, and a very competent-looking student staff was directing a production. The studio was connected directly with the stage of the auditorium, which was really at one end of an adjacent building. On the stage the director was rehearsing a play, but folding doors divided the auditorium so that other parts could be used at the same time. As we were ushered to the main entrance, we passed a group in one part taking a standardized test, and in another a debate rehearsal. From the foyer of the auditorium a covered passage led to the several laboratory workrooms for the different school subjects. In the shop and the home economics centers, our guide pointed out a number of machines he called *trainer units*. A student was sitting or standing at a table in front of each, watching a series of slides and listening to recorded directions which he followed by manipulating the material on the table. "These devices speed up learning of everything from dressmaking to automobile repair as much as 40 per cent," our guide explained. "The instructor as monitor helps them learn to generalize to similar processes."

As we followed our guide about, he kept up a steady stream of explanation, interrupted only by greetings and questions directed to staff members and students in the various rooms we visited. On our return to his office he picked up an earlier question about the years covered by the high school, pointing out that the expectations were different for different students.

Continuity

"One of the three basic principles of educational technology," he began, "is continuity—continuity in subject matter from the first steps to the most complex details, and continuity in the progression of students, as they grow older, in their mastery of knowledge and skills and the attainment of understanding. In the old days there was a kind of pseudo-continuity derived from testing children in different grades, but it presented many difficulties. Some time back, the ASCD got out a report [4] which showed that as the students saw it, there were four situations tending to interfere with their smooth progress through school—moving to a new school community, teacher behavior, subject matter, and moving to a new level. It was an excellent analysis but the authors did not consider the idea of eliminating the grade classification,

[4] The report to which he referred is the 1958 Yearbook of the Association for Supervision and Curriculum Development entitled, *A Look at Continuity in the School Program.*

and this was what was really responsible for most of the difficulties. More than a quarter of the children each year went to schools in a community that was new to them, and to fit these alone into some grade or other was quite a problem, to say nothing of the transfers within a school system. Some time later, the measurement people, stimulated by the possibilities of continuity in programming, began to work on the idea of a continuum of scores, with any one score depending not on a distribution of scores of any grade group but on the distance an individual has progressed, along a known course, whatever 'grade' he is in or however old he is. The average ages of students obtaining these scores is of some interest, but we do not regard them as norms.

"Now to get back to your question. Formerly this would have been called a six-year high school; but students are here from four to eight years, depending on their abilities, the programs they elect, and their vocational objectives. Some who enter are programmed for work which most of them have finished in the elementary school. The bright ones have already completed in elementary school what most of our students do here during their first and second years. But the progress of both is continuous. If they have taken French in the elementary school, they go right on with it here: they don't take it a year or two and then drop it and do something else. The same with other subjects."

Units of Achievement

"That sounds reasonable," we commented, "but aren't certain units in different subjects required for college entrance?"

"The Carnegie units!" he exploded. "Thank goodness we have got rid of them. When they became an issue, to our surprise nobody wanted to go to the mat for them. The colleges have found that our reports giving level of achievement instead of hours of sitting-time are more useful and fit into their computers just as well. So now a student can continue his French, for example, devoting a smaller amount of time a week to it, and begin to develop mastery in another language or in some other area. The whole trouble was that we thought in terms of courses. Yet nobody could say just what a course was, where it began, or where it ended."

Teaching Competence

"You spoke of continuity as one of the three basic principles of educational technology," we interposed. "What are the other two?"

"Teaching competence and adaptation to student ability," he replied. "They don't sound particularly new, do they? But now for the first time we can really do something about them. Take teaching competence. The programs, whether presented by machine or in book form, are prepared by experts and published only after lengthy tryout and revision. Our television programs likewise. And I might say that we do not pay expert teachers to sit with the students and watch kinescopes. The TV talent, monitors, homeroom teachers, directors, and discussion leaders are all especially chosen for their native ability and training."

Individual Differences

"And take adaptation to student ability," he continued. "Individual differences have been the shibboleth of educators for half a century, but all they could do was to try out various schemes for homogeneous grouping, all unsatisfactory. Pacing was just a word, but now, with the machine programs it is a reality. Occasionally we get a student from an old traditional school—there are still a few of them left—and you'd be surprised the way he reacts, once he gets the hang of the system. Maybe it's, 'You mean I don't have to poke along with the dumb bunnies,' or if he is down toward the other end, he comes up with something like, 'Now I see what they were talking about.' "

Which Medium to Use

"Does the systems approach raise the question as to which medium should be used for different subjects?" we inquired.

"Oh yes," the principal answered smiling, "we're still working on that one, and will be for some time, and also for what parts of each subject. In the earlier experiments, one school would use TV, another TM, and each medium would get a black eye because it did not usher in the millennium. As we see it, each has its possibilities including, you know, 'the living teacher'! But we have certain guide lines that help us decide."

"Do you mind revealing what they are?" we asked.

"Glad to," he responded, and started checking them off on his fingers. "First, use the medium that does the best job. That sounds obvious, but it keeps us from using a new medium just because it's new or an old one just because it's old. Second, use large class groups or projection and recordings for information that is to be given to large numbers of students instead of repeating it to different groups. This is just good economy. Third, explore the possibilities for using audio-visual materials. Teachers were so used to talking that it did not occur to them that films or tapes might do a better job. Even if they saw the possibilities, the projectors were a nuisance to locate and use. These are general; now to be more specific.

"Fourth, use films or TV for perceptual background, general orientation, and demonstration. Natural and social sciences and the arts seem to profit most. But you never know whether the students are soaking it up or letting it go by. A while back we tried out one of those devices that shoot in multiple-choice questions from time to time, and the students punches buttons for the answers. It may have possibilities. Some students liked it, others didn't. It was more of a distraction than a help. Fifth, use teaching machines or programmed texts when basic facts and concepts have to be learned. They are a natural supplement to films and TV. The students are all set to answer questions, as they are not when using TV materials, and the way the programming is done, they like it. And sixth, use supplementary readings all along. This is important so students will not become dependent on media they will not always find outside of school."

"How about originality and creativity?" we asked.

"Good programming can take care of that," he answered, "though many programs don't. But remember our first guideline, 'Use the medium that does the best job.' The best opportunities for originality and creativity are where they always were, in individual study, group discussion, and projects."

He paused for a moment, looking out the window where we could see some of the playground activities. "Our one remaining guideline, at least for the present," he continued, "is give practice in interpersonal skills. Examples are team sports, also music, dramatics, and discussion. Students can be taught nomenclature, rules, and general ideas effectively in other ways, but for doing with other people, experience is necessary, so we have our directors of such activities to help the students develop these group skills."

Dimensions of Learning

He leaned forward, his elbows on his desk. We thought he was deciding whether he would spend any more time on us, but since we made no move to leave, he began again. "You see, we have come to distinguish three dimensions of learning, and the distinctions not only clarify our objectives, but also partly determine the media we employ, and even our program of testing. One-dimensional learning, we call it Class 1, is linear, comparable to the improvement in track and field events—shorter time or greater distance as measured. In the school subjects, progress is from one item to the next, and each must be correct, and for this the Skinnerian programming is ideal. Almost any aspect of language study or mathematics and most athletic and vocational skills are in this category. Responses are either right or wrong. The patient tutoring offered by the machine produces and reinforces correct responses, and drills and corrects as no classroom teacher possibly can. It tells the kinds of mistakes students make so the monitors can administer first aid. Of course, film, books, and other materials are used to supplement the programmed instruction. In the linear dimension, proficiency is relatively easy to measure in terms of progress made. Marks are unnecessary, although comparisons with age norms are of interest as indicators of aptitude.

"Two-dimensional learning is appropriate for a general over-all view of an area, a surface knowledge of some of the main features and their relation to each other. We call this Class 2. Geography, history, and in fact the social sciences generally and most of the humanities are in this category. All agree that people should be informed in these areas, but with some exceptions there is little agreement on specific items or the order in which they should be learned, and individual interest is an important factor. For testing, the usual sampling of questions would be adequate. One can't know everything about everything, but attention can be given to significant facts and principles and to the relationships between them on the basis of which one gains what is referred to as background of knowledge or understanding. For this purpose, audio-visual materials are of first importance, including televised talks, explanations, and demonstrations. But these are supplemented by TM programs which develop the meaning of the new concepts, and of course by reading and discussion."

We could understand why our guide, now turned mentor, had paused before embarking on this elaboration of his ideas. In these two categories we saw the expert and the citizen taking shape. Surely the third man would be the scholar.

"The third dimension," he continued, after a moment's pause, "involves study and practice 'in depth' in more restricted areas. Three-dimensional learning, Class 3, is scholarship, what is expected of the more advanced students in college or graduate school, what is ridiculed as knowing more and more about less and less. In the secondary school we cannot expect to go very far in this dimension, but we follow it now and then. Any medium may be helpful at one point or another, but a good library is needed and a teacher who can suggest resources but otherwise keeps out of the student's way!"

He smiled as he said this, and we were sure that he had in mind some interesting cases, but we had already trespassed too long on his good nature. At the door we tossed out one final question, "Do you sometimes yearn for the simpler days of old, with one teacher to each classroom?"

He looked as if he had been struck in the face. "Good heavens, no!" he exclaimed. This is what we thought he would say, but we wanted to hear him say it. When he saw our smile, he laughed, waved farewell, and the door closed. As we started our car, we remembered our visit to the elementary school: "It makes sense, and it works."

HIGHER EDUCATION

Change Is Gradual

Experimental studies have been carried on in the colleges and universities with the support of federal and foundation grants. But as in the lower schools, each has usually sought to explore the possibilities of some one of the new media, and a systems approach seems a long ways away. In spite of the fact that television instruction has featured the lecture, college lectures have continued as before, except as a few institutions have broadcast to neighboring ones, or as lectures have been polished up with the aid of teleprompter and multiple screens. And in one university, at least, a central projection service has been expanded to permit an instructor in a given classroom to pre-arrange for a given film or kinescope to be fed to his classroom from a central projection room elsewhere in the building. The instructor pushes buttons which start, stop, or reverse the film as he sees fit during his lecture. But from such points it is difficult to extrapolate far enough to discover the future of educational technology in colleges and universities. A few straws in the wind, however, may be interpreted or misinterpreted as follows.

The Carnegie unit will disappear and students will be admitted on the basis of proficiency. Progress from high school to college will be continuous for each subject, but various cutting points will be established. Thus high school work will not be repeated in college, and each student will start in college where he left off in high school. Not only will the cutting point be more clearly defined, but it will be farther along the line of subject matter competence than heretofore. For example, language competence may be a condition of admission. Instead of depending on dubious marks on student transcripts, and their correlation with equally dubious college marks, rather specific data on their achievement will be made available. Perhaps their position on the 1000-point scale will be the basis for admission. In doubtful cases students may receive credit by examination, as is done here and there today, without necessarily having to sit through a specified number of hours in a college classroom. Examination scores, together with a record of programmed learning completed, will be sufficient. What will become of courses and credit hours it is impossible to discern, since that portion of the crystal ball is badly smudged.

Television and Teaching Machines

Separate sections of large classes will be connected by television, and this medium will be increasingly used for lecture demonstrations and for the observation of relevant outside events. A TV camera can not only show dissections clearly to a large group, but attached to a microscope it will present the same magnification to all. At least one court room has been connected by CCTV with a law school lecture hall, and education students have been enabled to observe school classroom procedures in another building. Much elementary and intermediate level instruction in all areas will be provided by the new media. A valuable refresher service has already been provided by scrambled books. One physics professor, for example, has developed informal programs in geometry and trigonometry by means of which students who so desire may review the parts of those subjects needed in the physics course. With the use of the new media there can be greater emphasis on independent study and on group discussion. The seminar, a distinctly university invention, will probably have greater prominence as staff members are relieved of some of their lecturing responsibilities.

As kinescopes and teaching machine programs are developed, it will be less necessary for students to attend campus classes. Many of the courses as now known will wither away, and students living in the most remote areas will receive the same instruction as those on the campus. This suggestion holds out interesting possibilities not only for campus housing, but also for the changed role of the extension teacher who may well become a kind of field secretary.

TEACHER EDUCATION

Teacher-training institutions will for some time have a dual responsibility. They must prepare their graduates to operate both with the old and the new technology, and they must incorporate the new media into their instructional program wherever they would presumably effect an improvement. There is little doubt that once the responsibility is seriously undertaken, and a careful appraisal is made of the instructional program in higher education, as in the lower schools, the need for many long-overdue changes will be recognized. Programming will reveal the extent of overlapping content in different courses more clearly than heretofore, and will suggest the desirability of credit by examination. This will reveal the fallacies of the credit hour as a unit of measurement of learning content, and will also tend to promote independent study. Television will suggest possibilities of improving lecture demonstrations and point up the necessity for group discussions and participation. In addition it will do much to correct two of the greatest weaknesses of the present professional training program. One of these is the inadequate provision for observation of and participation in schoolroom practices. The other is the generally unsatisfactory condition of off-campus (extension) instruction.

It will no doubt be some time before teacher-training institutions can give their students the benefits that experience with instruction by the new media can bring. But meanwhile, their graduates in increasing numbers will be securing positions in schools where the new technology is already at various stages of development. The first step has already been taken in a number of institutions, that of adding new courses and workshops, primarily for teachers in service, to train them in the use of the new media and to furnish consulting services. The next step, unfortunately, if experience is any indication, will be to present the same content in a number of different education courses. If the period of such duplication can be shortened, it should be possible early to incorporate the training and experience all should have in a common core of instruction. The purpose will be to provide a general understanding of the technological approach that should make for flexibility of adaptation to the immediate situation and to future change. Such a common core can then be supplemented by different kinds of specialized experience with the new media.

The practice teaching for the generalist will thus gradually be supplemented by practicums and internships providing work experience as a medium of instruction, and for the specialists by training in one kind of job or another in the man-machine systems of the schools of the future.

Exploration of the possibilities of the new technology should also lead to a clearer identification of the roles of specialists in education and in content subjects with a great deal more collaboration than has been common in the past. It may even be that the competence of school staff members in both their professional and their subject matter specializations will be developed, and be judged on the basis of their achievements and proficiency instead of the number of credit hours they have accumulated.

In Conclusion

EDUCATIONAL TECHNOLOGY may now be defined more completely as continuing changes in educational procedures growing out of applied scientific research at the points where theory and practice meet, and resulting in increasing precision in the control of environmental factors through the coordinated action of personnel and instructional media in a man-machine system in the interest of more effective learning. The manufacturers of the hardware are no doubt speeding the change, seeing, as some do, the possibility of a hundred-million-dollar market. The new devices, the possible uses of which are being energetically explored by industry and the armed forces, have presented a challenge to educators which they cannot afford to ignore, particularly at the present juncture.

THE PRESSURES ON THE SCHOOLS

Constrictive and Developmental Pressures

More students are crowding into the schools than ever before, each one of whom deserves individual attention, but they find themselves in larger and larger classes or even on part time. Special certificates are being issued to untrained teachers because there are not enough who have the proper preparation, and both the children and the public at large are the losers. There are not only more students and hence too few good teachers, but there is relatively less money for education, which results in proportionately less schoolroom space and fewer teachers.

These downward constrictive pressures are met by upward pressures for the development and improvement of the school program. And the schools are caught between. Many wish to retain students in school longer, to provide new buildings, a more enriched curriculum, better teaching, a larger proportion of graduates who are trained in the disciplines, less disturbed mentally, less inclined to delinquency, and more competent professionally. The pressure for excellence demands that the schools satisfy the intellectual and cultural needs not only in mathematics, the sciences, and the humanities, but in producing good citizens.

It is a kind of squeeze play the public is using on the schools, as a consequence of which they can do one of two things. They can either continue in their traditional ways to struggle along, or they can streamline their operations, and taking advantage of the present interest and concern, introduce the necessary innovations.

Change in a Dynamic Society

In a static society, change is anathema, but there seem to be few if any static societies left in the world today. There are only minority segments that can be so classified, and it is to be hoped that education is not among them. It has certainly not been static during the past hundred years or so, which have seen the change from the narrow, classical curriculum to the elective system, the development of the problem and project methods, the introduction of art and vocational courses into the curriculum, the use of standardized tests, the growth of psychological counseling, and the spread of programs for special education for the handicapped, to say nothing of the rise of the junior high school that carried many of these changes with it, the rapid consolidation of one-room district schools, and as a kind of symbol of all these things, the easily observable improvements that have been made in school architecture.

Most of the innovations, after undergoing various modifications, have become so much a matter of common practice that many younger people today cannot imagine anything different. In the military phrase, they have become standard operating procedure.

DIRECTIONS OF CHANGE

But change can hardly be expected to stop now. Certainly no education paradise has yet been attained, if the more vocal critics of the schools are to be believed. Even if some of the solutions they propose for educational problems cannot be taken too seriously, they sometimes point to weaknesses which have long been recognized, but which hitherto have been impossible to correct. If a specific proposal was put forward, there was nothing to take care of it in the budget, something else had priority, the time was not ripe, it would disturb the smooth-running of the school, parents would object, and so on. But now things are different. There is ferment in the air. Innovations are being tried, changes are being made. The climate is different. The time is ripe.

The Tasks Ahead

No one can say just what any individual school or school system should do first. A number of suggestions have already been made. It may be that besides specific proposals it would be well to get a kind of over-all view of the tasks ahead. First, there are the great unmet needs of education. It is estimated that some 5 million Americans are functionally illiterate, that the little reading and writing they can do is insufficient to be of any use to them personally or vocationally. Thousands of previously employed men and women have been displaced not only by automation but also by new inventions. By new methods, many more of them than in the past might be retrained for other jobs or upgraded to a skilled or semi-skilled category. Overseas, illiteracy varies widely, and fundamental, preliterate education and technical training are needed in many of the industrially underdeveloped countries. Everywhere there is a demand for knowledge of a second and even a third language, and everywhere new skills are needed and new knowledge sought. The old teacher-class method is totally inadequate in view of present conditions. The new methods hold the promise of success that without them would be quite impossible to achieve.

Within the American school system, another group of tasks may be classified as clearing out the obsolescent procedures, the place for which is in a museum, not in the school of the future. Actually, they are not educational procedures; although they have long been associated with education, there is no necessary connection. They are just the old-fashioned *modus operandi* which will no longer be needed.

Student Classification

First there is the outmoded system of student classification to be got rid of. Grade rooms, promotion policies, and teachers' marks all imply a fiction that has little or no basis in fact. That the system has not exploded long since is evidence of the ingenuity and devotion of the teachers who have been required to employ it. To force children of widely different abilities to work at the same intellectual tasks has been little short of madness. The effort to fit each to the Procrustean beds in each grade room has been eminently unsuccessful as evidenced by the varying promotion policies of different schools where teachers must decide how many of the children to "fail" because they did not do what they did not have the ability to do, and how many to "pass" on the false assumption that they all earned their promotion. That it is a false assumption is revealed clearly by the marking system showing the low level of ability of many who are passed, who are quite unprepared to do "the work of the next grade," while others were ready several weeks or months earlier. So with the banishment of grade grouping and promotion can also go the time-consuming and partially fraudulent activity of marking. The fraud has long since been exposed by numerous studies of differences in the marks of different teachers of the same pupils, and by the analyses of the nature of the value judgments made, including the varying criteria employed.

Achievement Units

Along with grades, promotion, and marks will go the artificial units by which achievement is measured, the packaging of accomplishment in standard-length courses, credit hours, and any other measures built on the assumption that the degree of mastery of any subject matter can be adequately measured by the amount of time spent in hearing it expounded. As has been noted, the Carnegie unit is now used for a purpose for which it was never intended. The fixed, year-length, five-day-a-week courses limit the number of subjects students may take because an equal amount of class time must be spent on each by all students whether or not they need it, or the subject matter warrants it. A "course" has no definable beginning, middle, or end in terms of either time or content. It is a pleasing fiction, since if one has had it, presumably he has had something, but no one knows just what, nor even with his marks nicely reproduced on his transcript can any one ascertain what he knows. The confusion is bad enough in the secondary school, but in college it is thrice confounded. Courses with different names may be practically identical, and those with the same name quite different, while the same mark indicates varying degrees of excellence from college to college and even from instructor to instructor in the same institution.

Of course, all this old machinery cannot be thrown out the window at once. The result would be chaos, not much greater than we have at the present time, perhaps, but a chaos no one would be able to handle. The kind of genius that has built up the present industrial civilization and seeks to explore outer space should not quail at the thought of making the needed changes—substituting individualized instruction and like groups for the present miscellaneous heterogeneity; continued progress for sporadic course selections and arbitrary promotions; valid and reliable scores for subjective marks; objectively defined increments in complexity in knowledge and skill for the anomalous courses; and comparable units indicating degree of competence for credit hours and honor points.

"The" Classroom Teacher

The teacher and *the* classroom (usually "her" classroom in spite of the large number of men in the profession) seem to constitute the *sine qua non* of the educational enterprise. Are these also to be sacrificed on the altar of the new technology? The answer is, of course, an unqualified *No.* But as the words are usually employed, they represent a stereotype that will have to be broken if education is to move ahead as it is already possible to do. In fact, the stereotype is already badly cracked. The original was the schoolmaster, who used to be the only adult found in the school building. But now there are on the payroll superintendents, principals, supervisors, librarians, curriculum specialists, audio-visualists, psychologists, social workers, examiners, counselors, attendance officers, bus drivers, custodians, and others. In a sense they are all teachers, but they are not all called teachers.

The varying roles noted earlier of those who are called teachers, present an impossible array of responsibilities that no one person, however gifted, can play successfully, although many do surprisingly well. Further differentiation of labor is required by the new technology. The school personnel will be teachers, but no one of them will be *the* teacher. The word *classroom* is a similar stereotype in spite of the fact that there is no longer just one room for all, as in the days of the schoolmaster. Even now, in addition to so-called regular classrooms, there are gymnasiums, practice rooms, cafeterias, laboratories, libraries, shops, auditoriums, and multi-purpose rooms. It is only natural that educational technology should call for further modifications in school architecture for form should follow function. There will of course be rooms for children and young people to meet singly and in groups of different sizes. But no one of them will be *the* classroom.

INSTRUCTION AND LEARNING

All this, however, is but the form, the shell, the container. What is done by the school personnel in the different kinds of rooms is the important thing. A rough sketch of some of the possibilities has been presented in this volume. What will be done in any one school system presents an exciting challenge to the personnel now operating in it. Planning, caution, and foresight are essential, but so are courage and daring. And good as some schools are, there is little doubt but that any changes made will be for the better. It is hard to realize that the children who are in the schools today will be attending the schools of "tomorrow." Most of those who enter kindergarten in 1962 will not finish high school until 1975, and they will be only forty-five years old, in the prime of life, in the year 2000. In a sense, their future is now. It is for that future that we must plan, not for the present or past century.

No one can predict the curricular changes that will be needed in the years to come, but we can be reasonably certain that communication skills through the proper use of words and numbers will always be necessary, if for no other reason than for the introduction they provide for everything else, for concepts of space and time, size and causality, as a basis for understanding planet Earth and perhaps its neighbors, and meeting the many problems, large and small, which it presents to us and will continue to present. It is just possible that in the future not only the masses of people, but the elite of one kind or another as well, can be so educated as to be less prone to confuse causal with temporal sequences, to derive fallacious conclusions from untenable generalizations, and to accept such conclusions without question when they are in agreement with their own irrational prejudices. The addition of the new media to our resources, with the more adequate control of the learning environment that they provide, makes such a possibility far less remote than it has ever been before. But automation will not do it automatically. The educational hardware, like the electronic computers, is dependent on the data that are fed into them. There are and will be many ineffectual programs, both TV and TM, and the results of any adventures with the new media should be judged accordingly. But now as never before the way is open to provide the kinds of instruction that are needed to obtain educational objectives sought. Rationalizing the teaching-learning processes, as implied by the term *educational technology,* makes it possible to do the following things more effectively than ever before.

Adaptation to the Learner

Adapt instruction to the abilities of the learner. Programmed learning breaks up the traditional lockstep and makes individualized instruction a reality. The learner works at educational tasks that are on the level with his abilities and proceeds at the rate at which he is capable of proceeding.

Adapt instruction to the individual needs of the learner. The possibilities for greater flexibility allow for the enrichment of curricular content by branching and other techniques in accord with the student's vocational or other interests. And since no one has to "keep up with the class," disturbed students can be given the psychological attention they need, and pressures can be temporarily reduced, and help given while personality adjustments are made.

Adaptation to Content

Adapt instruction to the requirements of the content being taught. Instead of teaching all subjects in much the same way with the teacher up in front talking to the class and with only occasional individual or group participation, perceptual content, demonstration, drill, discussion, independent study, and so on can each be more effectively handled in appropriate ways. And they can take whatever time the content requires, different for different students, instead of being crowded together or stretched out to fit into a year-long course. Duplication of content can be restricted to what is desired for review purposes instead of being allowed to run rampant.

Control of Environment

Control the teaching environment more satisfactorily than heretofore. Such control is implied in what has been said above, but here the emphasis is on breaking up the system which gives almost absolute control of children for a whole year, either in an elementary grade or in a high school course, to one teacher who may be good, bad, or indifferent.

Continuity

Provide continuity from year to year for each student, who begins each school year where he left off the year before, and for each subject so that he will not have to drop it in order to take another to meet some arbitrary requirement. Foreign language study is a good example. Shop, art, and music might not need to be alternative choices.

The question has earlier been raised as to the meaning of

the word *course*. Webster defines it as "a unit of instruction consisting of recitations, lectures, laboratory, experiments, and the like in a particular subject." But what is a unit of instruction! When or where should a course begin or end? What does it mean to "cover a course"? Actually, as now used, *course* seems to mean an artificially delineated fragment of a subject, the boundaries being determined by the supposed competence of the average student, the content being defined by a textbook and/or the amount of talking in class that a teacher feels like doing. Perhaps it is possible to do better than this. There might be value in the following definition: logically or meaningfully related content arranged in order of increasing complexity, in the comprehension of which a student may be expected to make continuous progress toward mastery at his own optimum rate. It then becomes an arrangement of subject matter, a line along which a student progresses, and is determined by the progress he makes. This definition still leaves questions of selection and depth of exploration to be decided, as they are now, but it avoids assuming any age or grade determination.

The Learning Process

Lastly, and applicable throughout, harmonize instruction with what is known of the nature of the learning process. Appropriate media and procedures can be provided for the child as a dynamic organism, enriching his perceptual experiences, developing an understanding of the meaning of new concepts and their relationships, providing practices in problem solving, and improving linguistic, motor, and social skills. The varied media, new and old, that are best adapted to each of these processes can now be chosen for the specific contribution each can make. And further, programmed instruction insures a more perfect coverage for each student than was previously possible, and employs the feedback and reinforcement necessary for learning.

EDUCATIONAL TECHNOLOGY AND SYSTEMS

It is no doubt evident that no explosive educational revolution is imminent, but that the rate of evolutionary change is accelerating. Further, it is evident, at least in the author's opinion, that the millennium for education will not be ushered in by the purchase of a truckload of teaching machines and another of television equipment. The new media provide the occasion for overhauling educational machinery, for throwing out what is ineffective and even detrimental, but for retaining what is good and necessary.

The new media will not be particularly effective so long as they remain mere aids or adjuncts, an intrusion, a fifth wheel to the educational conveyance. The new parts need to be integrated into a man-machine system, and this requires clearcut readjustments in organization and procedure. The required changes may take a little time but they are well within the range of feasibility. The educational technologist envisions not machine-produced robots, but a smoothly functioning system in which the several processes it employs are all operating to turn out its product—and that product is educated people. It is not realistic to expect that the product will be perfect. But the schools of tomorrow can be far better places to live and to learn than the schools of today.

Bibliography

AID for Education and Training. Institute of International Research and Development, Lubbock, Texas, 5 (September, 1961), 43.

Allen, William H., *Television for California Schools.* Bulletin of the California State Department of Education, Vol. 39, No. 4 (April, 1960). 48 pp.

And No Bells Ring. National Association of Secondary School Principals, 1961. 57-minute film on large-group instruction, small-group discussion, independent study, and the teacher team. Address: 1201 Sixteenth Street, N.W., Washington, D.C.

Association for Supervision and Curriculum Development, *A Look at Continuity in the School Program.* 1958 Yearbook, National Education Association, 1958.

AV Communication Review. Special Supplement, Redefinition and Terminology, Washington Department of AV Instruction, National Education Association.

Barnes, Virginia C., *The Organization and Administration of the Instructional Materials Center in Medium-Sized School Districts.* Doctoral Thesis, Stanford University, 1960, 247 pp. Abstract: Dissertation Abstracts 21: 1104-1105.

Besvinck, Sidney L., "The Expendable Carnegie Unit." *Phi Delta Kappan,* 42 (May, 1961), 356-366.

Bloom, Benjamin S., ed., *Taxonomy of Educational Objectives— The Classification of Educational Goals.* New York, Longmans, Green & Co., 1956.

Brethower, Dale M., *Programmed Instruction and Programming Techniques—The Analysis of an Educational Technology.* Ann Arbor, The Institute for Behavioral Research and Programmed Instruction, 1962. (A program on programming.)

Brinkmann, Erwin H., *Educability in Visualization of Objects in Space: A Programmed Instruction Approach.* Doctoral Thesis, The University of Michigan, Ann Arbor, 1963.

Carpenter, C. R., "Approaches to Promising Areas of Research in the Field of Instructional Television." New Teaching Aids for the American Classroom. Stanford, Calif., Institute for Communications Research, 1960. Pp. 73-94.

Carpenter, C. R., and others, *An Investigation of Closed-Circuit Television for Teaching University Courses.* University Park, The Pennsylvania State University, Research Division of Academic Research Services, 1958.

Carpenter, Finley, *Teaching Machines and Programmed Instruction.* Syracuse: The Library of Education, Center for Applied Research in Education, Inc., 1963.

Cartwright, Dorwin and Zander, Alvin, eds., *Group Dynamics Research and Theory,* 2d ed. New York, Harper & Row, Publishers, 1960.

Cassirer, Henry, *Television Teaching Today.* New York, UNESCO Publications Center of Columbia University Press, 1961.

Clinchy, Evans, ed., *Profiles of Significant Schools—Schools for Team Teaching.* New York, Educational Facilities Laboratories, 477 Madison Ave., 1961.

Cogswell, John F. in *Aid for Education and Training.* Lubbock (Tex.), Institute of International Research and Development (September, 1961), p. 43.

Commission on the Reorganization of Secondary Education, *Cardinal Principles of Secondary Education.* U.S. Office of Education, Bull. 35, 1918.

Conant, James B., "Another Look at the Comprehensive High School." *NEA Journal,* 51 (May, 1962), 29-31.

Coulson, John E., ed., *Programmed Learning and Computer-Based Instruction.* Proceedings of the Conference on Application of Digital Computers to Automated Instruction, Oct. 10–12, 1961. New York, John Wiley & Sons, Inc., 1962.

Cram, David, *Explaining Teaching Machines and Programming.* San Francisco, Fearon Publishers, Inc., 1961.

Cronbach, Lee J., *Essentials of Psychological Testing.* New York, Harper & Row, Publishers, 1960. Pp. 385-388.

Crowder, Norman A., "Automatic Tutoring by Intrinsic Programming." In A. A. Lumsdaine and Robert Glaser, eds., *Teaching Machines and Programmed Learning* (Washington, National Education Association, 1960), pp. 286-298.

————, "Automatic Tutoring by Means of Intrinsic Programming." In E. H. Galanter, ed., *Automatic Teaching: The State of the Art* (New York, John Wiley & Sons, Inc., 1959), pp. 109-116.

————, "Intrinsically Programmed Materials for Teaching Complex Skills and Concepts." Paper read at the American Psychological Association, Washington, D.C. (August, 1958).

Cunningham, Luvern C., "Team Teaching: Where Do We Stand?" *Administrator's Notebook,* Midwest Administration Center, The University of Chicago, Vol. 8, No. 8 (April, 1960).

Dale, Edgar, "No Room for Amateurs." *Audio-Visual Instruction* 6 (May, 1961), 190-192.

Davis, O. L., Jr., "Textbooks and Other Printed Materials." *Review of Educational Research* 32 (April, 1962), Chap. 2.

DeBernardis, Amo, and others, in cooperation with the U.S. Office of Education, *Planning Schools for the New Media.* Division of Education, Portland State College, Portland, Oregon, 1961.

de Kieffer, Robert E., *Audio-Visual Education.* Syracuse, The Library of Education, Center for Applied Research in Education, Inc., 1963.

Department of Public Instruction, *Planning the Instructional Materials Center.* Bull. 422, 1958; *Staffing the Instructional Materials Center.* Bull. 427, 1960; *The Instructional Materials Center in Action.* Bull. 429, Lansing, Michigan, The Department, 55 pp.

Deterline, William J., *An Introduction to Programed Instruction.* Englewood Cliffs, N.J., Prentice-Hall, Inc., 1962.

Eboch, Sidney C., *Operating Audio-Visual Equipment.* San Francisco, Chandler Publishing Co., 1960.

Epstein, Sam and Beryl, *The First Book of Teaching Machines.*
New York, Franklin Watts, Inc., 1961.

Fearing, Franklin, "Social Impact of the Mass Media of Communication," *Mass Media and Education.* Fifty-third Yearbook
of the National Society for the Study of Education, Part II.
Chicago, University of Chicago Press, 1954.

Finch, G., ed., *Symposium on Educational and Training Media.*
Washington, National Academy of Sciences, National Research Council, 1960.

Finn, James D., "A Look at the Future of AV Communication."
Audio-visual Communication Review, 8 (Winter, 1960),
5-26. Also "Automation and Education: III. Technology and
the Instructional Process." *ibid.*

Finn, James D., *Teacher Education—Direction for the Sixties.*
Tenth Biennial Survey for Executives, Bemidji State College,
1961.

Finn, James D. and Perrin, Donald G., *Teaching Machines and
Programmed Learning, 1962: A Survey of the Industry.* Oc-
casional Paper No. 3, N. E. A. Technological Development
Project. Washington, National Education Association, 1961.

Fitts, Paul M., "Humans in Man-Machine Systems." *Research
News,* The University of Michigan, 13 (July 1, 1962), 1-4.

Foltz, Charles I., *The World of Teaching Machines, Programmed
Learning and Self-Instruction.* Washington, Electronic Teaching Laboratories, Teaching Research and Technology Division, 1961.

French, Will and associates, *Behavior Goals of General Education in High School.* New York, Russell Sage Foundation,
1957.

Gage, N. L., ed., *Handbook of Research in Teaching.* Washington, American Educational Research Association, National
Education Association, 1962.

Gagné, Robert M., ed., *Psychological Principles in System Development.* New York, Holt, Rinehart and Winston, Inc., 1962.

Galanter, Eugene H., ed., *Automatic Teaching: The State of the
Art.* New York, John Wiley & Sons, Inc., 1959.

Glaser, Robert, ed., *Training Research and Education.* Pittsburgh,
University of Pittsburgh Press, 1962.

Goodlad, John I. and Anderson, Robert H., *The Nongraded Elementary School.* New York, Harcourt, Brace & World, Inc., 1959.

Green, Edward J., *The Learning Process and Programmed Instruction.* New York, Holt, Rinehart and Winston, Inc., 1962.

Hauf, Harold D., and others, *New Spaces for Learning.* Troy, N.Y., School of Architecture, Rensselaer Polytechnic Institute, 1961. 79 pp. plus design studies.

Homme, L. E., and Glaser, R., "Problems in Programming Verbal Learning Sequences," in *Teaching Machines and Programmed Learning, A Service Book.* Washington, National Education Association, 1960.

Homme, L. E., and Glaser, R., "Relationship between the Programmed Textbook and Teaching Machines." Paper presented at the conference on Automatic Teaching of Verbal and Symbolic Skills, University of Pennsylvania, 1958.

Huebner, Theodore, *Audio-Visual Techniques in Teaching Foreign Languages.* New York, New York University Press, 1960.

Hughes, J. L., *Programed Instruction for Schools and Industry.* Chicago, Science Research Associates, 1962.

Hunter, Armand L., *Educational TV.* Syracuse, The Library of Education, Center for Applied Research in Education, Inc., 1962.

Hutchinson, Joseph C., *Modern Foreign Languages in High School —The Language Laboratory.* U.S. Office of Education, Bull. 1961, No. 23, 1961.

Johnson, Marjorie C., and Remer, Ilo, *References on Foreign Languages in the Elementary School.* U.S. Office of Education Circular No. 495, rev., 1959.

Klaus, David J., "The Art of Instructional Programming," in Wendel I. Smith and J. William Moore, eds., *Programmed Learning* (New York, D. Van Nostrand Co., Inc., 1962).

Learning and Behavior. 26-minute film, B. F. Skinner's Psychological Laboratory. New York, Carousel Films, Inc.

Lewis, Lanora G., "The Credit System in Colleges and Universities." U.S. Office of Education, Division of Higher Education: New Dimensions in Higher Education, Bul. 9, 1961.

Lewis, Philip, *Education Television Guide Book*. New York, Mc-
Graw-Hill Book Co., Inc., 1961.

Lippitt, Ronald, and others, *The Dynamics of Planned Change*.
New York, Harcourt, Brace & World, Inc., 1958.

Lumsdaine, A. A., "Graphic Aids, Models and Mockups as Tools
for Individual and Classroom Instruction," in G. Finch,
ed., *Symposium on Educational and Training Media* (Washington, National Academy of Sciences-National Research
Council, 1960).

———, "Instruments and Media of Instruction," in N. L. Gage,
ed., *Handbook of Research in Teaching* (Washington, National Education Association, 1962).

———, and Glaser, Robert, eds., *Teaching Machines and Programmed Learning: A Source Book*. Washington, Department of Audio-Visual Instruction, National Education Association, 1960.

Lysaught, Jerome P., *Programmed Learning*. Ann Arbor, Michigan, Foundation for Research on Human Behavior, 1961.

Mager, Robert E., *Preparing Objectives for Programmed Instruction*. San Francisco, Fearon Publishers, Inc., 1961.

Markle, S. M., Eigen, L. D., and Komoski, P. K., *A Programed
Primer on Programing,* Vols. I and II. New York, The Cen-
ter for Programed Instruction, 1961. Also, *Words*. New
York, The Center for Programed Instruction, 1962.

Marley, Harold P., "When Humanism Becomes a Religion." *The
Humanist* IV (Spring, 1944), 24-26.

Mass Communication and Education, report of the Educational
Policies Commission. Washington, National Education Association, 1958.

Mathieu, Gustave, "Language Laboratories." *Review of Educational Research,* 32 (April, 1962), Chap. 5.

Mauch, James, "A Systems Analysis Approach to Education."
Phi Delta Kappan, 43 (January, 1962), 158-162.

Miller, Neal E., and others, "Graphic Communication and the
Crisis in Education." *Audio-Visual Communication Review,*
Vol. 5, No. 3 (1957), 1-120.

Miller, Robert B., "Analysis and Specification of Behavior for
Training," in Robert Glaser, ed., *Training Research and*

Education (Pittsburgh, University of Pittsburgh Press, 1962). Also, "Task Description and Analysis," in Robert M. Gagné, ed., *Psychological Principles in System Development* (New York, Holt, Rinehart and Winston, Inc., 1962).

Morse, Arthur D., *Schools of Tomorrow—Today*. A Report on Educational Experiments. Garden City, N.Y., Doubleday & Company, Inc., 1960.

National Association of Secondary School Principals, *Locus on Change—Staff Utilization Studies*. National Education Association, Bull. Vol. 46, No. 270 (January, 1962).

National Education Association, Educational Policies Commission, *Mass Communication and Education*. Washington, The Commission, 1958.

"New Educational Trends and Media—Their Impact on School Libraries." *ALA Bulletin* (February, 1961).

New Teaching Aids for the American Classroom. Symposium on the state of research in instructional TV and tutorial machines. Stanford University, California, Institute for Communication Research, 1959.

Orwell, George, *1984*. New York, Harcourt, Brace & World, Inc., 1949.

Pressey, S. L. See Lumsdaine and Glaser, *op. cit.* pp. 35-51, 69-88, 497-505.

Review of Educational Research, 32 (April, 1962).

Rigney, Joseph W., and Fry, Edward B., *Current Teaching Machine Programs and Programming Techniques*. Washington, Department of Audio-Visual Instruction, National Education Association, 1962.

Rogers, C. R., and Skinner, B. F., "Some Issues Concerning the Control of Human Behavior—a Symposium." *Science*, 124 (November 30, 1956), 1060-1064.

Silberman, Charles E., "The Remaking of American Education." *Fortune* (April, 1961), 3-11.

Silberman, Harry F., "Self-Teaching Devices and Programmed Materials." *Review of Educational Research*, 32 (April 1962), Chap. VI.

Skinner, B. F., "The Science of Learning and the Art of Teaching." *Harvard Educational Review*, 24 (Spring 1954), pp.

86-97. Also in Lumsdaine and Glaser, *op. cit.* pp. 99-113. See also in Lumsdaine and Glaser, "Teaching Machines," pp. 137-158.

————, *Verbal Behavior.* New York, Appleton-Century-Crofts, 1957.

————, *Walden Two.* New York, The Macmillan Company, 1948.

Smith, Wendell I., and Moore, J. William, eds., *Programmed Learning.* New York, D. Van Nostrand Co., Inc., 1962. Especially James G. Holland, "Principles from the Laboratory," 3-48, and David J. Klaus, "The Art of Auto-instructional Programming." 89-107.

Spaulding, William E., *Look to the School,* R. R. Bowker Memorial Lecture. New York, The New York Public Library. Reprinted by Houghton Mifflin Co., 1960.

Spencer, Herbert, *Education: Intellectual, Moral, Physical.* New York, D. Appleton and Company, 1861.

Spranger, Eduard, *Types of Men.* Halle, Max Niemeyer, 1928.

Stoddard, Alexander J., *Schools for Tomorrow.* New York, The Fund for the Advancement of Education, 1957.

Stoddard, George D., *The Dual Progress Plan.* New York, Harper & Row, Publishers, 1961.

Stolurow, Lawrence M., *Teaching by Machine.* U.S. Office of Education, Cooperative Research Monograph No. 6, 1961, p. 173.

Tarbet, Donald G., *Television and Our Schools.* New York, The Ronald Press Co., 1961.

Teacher Education—Direction for the Sixties. Tenth Biennial School for Executives, Bemidji State College. Washington, The American Association for Colleges for Teacher Education, 1961.

Thelen, Herbert A., *Education and the Human Quest.* New York, Harper & Row, Publishers, 1960.

Tompkins, Ellsworth, and Gaumnitz, Walter, *The Carnegie Unit: Its Origin, Status, and Trends.* U.S. Department of Health, Education and Welfare, Bull. 1954, No. 7, 1954.

Trump, Lloyd J., and Baynham, Dorsey, *Focus on Change— Guide to Better Schools.* Chicago, Rand McNally & Co., 1961.

Wagner, Robert W., "Design in Education." *The News Letter,* The Bureau of Educational Research and Service, Ohio State University, 27 (October, 1961), 1-4.

Wendt, Paul R., and Butts, Gordon K., "Audio-visual Materials." *Review of Educational Research,* 32 (April, 1962), Chap. III.

Woolman, Myron, *Programming for Conceptual Understanding.* A report to the Communication Social Science Research Department of The Bell Telephone Laboratories. Institute of Educational Research, 2226 Wisconsin Ave., N.W., Washington, D.C., undated (monolithed).

Index